The Chameleonic Learner
Learning and self-assessment in context

Roseanna Bourke

NZCER PRESS
Wellington 2010

NZCER PRESS
New Zealand Council for Educational Research
PO Box 3237
Wellington
New Zealand

© Roseanna Bourke, 2010

ISBN 978-1-877398-61-2

All rights reserved

Designed by Cluster Creative

Printed by Printlink, Wellington

Cover illustration:
A chameleon, 1612(?), Ustad Mansur (fl.c.1590-1630),
The Royal Collection © 2010 Her Majesty Queen Elizabeth II.
Reproduced with permission.

Distributed by NZCER Distribution Services
PO Box 3237
Wellington
New Zealand
www.nzcer.org.nz

Contents

Acknowledgements	**7**
Foreword	**9**
Preface	**11**
CHAPTER 1 The colour of learning: Why student voice is essential to personalising learning	**17**
Changing colour through learning	18
The personalised learning agenda: Its genesis and relevance	20
Personalised learning or just plain learning?	22
Observing the chameleonic learner: Ways to explore learning through student voice	24
Linking theories of learning to "everyday" learning	25
Students' conceptions of learning	26
Assessment agendas	27
Students' conceptions of self-assessment	28
Assessment and learning in context	29
Making choices about learning	30
CHAPTER 2 Changing the way we see student learning	**33**
Teacher as researcher	33
The study in brief	35
Discussing learning with students	36
What do you mean?	38
Listening for the metaphors	41
Observing in the classroom	41
Observing outside the classroom	43
Bringing to the fore what is to be analysed	44
Summary	45

CHAPTER 3 Learning: It's what we do — 47

Theoretical understandings of learning — 48
    Classical theory — 48
    Behavioural theories — 49
    Cognitive theories — 50
    Sociocultural theory — 51

Approaches to learning — 54
    Phenomenography — 54
    Learning and context — 57
    School learning — 59
    The role of peers in the learning process — 60
    Out-of-school learning — 61

Summary — 63

CHAPTER 4 Students and their learning — 65

Studying students' conceptions of learning — 66

Students' conceptions of learning — 66
    Acquiring knowledge (A): What do I need to know? — 69
    Memorising and reproducing (B): What do I need to remember? — 71
    Using your knowledge (C): How do I do this? — 75
    Understanding (D): How do I use this information? — 80
    Different ways of knowing (E): How can I solve this problem? — 85

Summary — 87

CHAPTER 5 Assessment and self-assessment — 91

Assessment: Roles, functions, influence — 92
Assessment: The political context — 96
Assessment as a dividing practice — 98
Self-assessment and lifelong learning: Sustainable assessment — 101
Incorporating self-assessment in teaching and learning — 104
Summary — 106

CHAPTER 6 How do students know when they have learnt?   **109**

Studying students' conceptions of self-assessment   111
    Seeking an opinion (A): Have I learnt?   114
    Getting marks and grades (B): How much have I learnt?   117
    Performing (C): What did I learn?   121
    Using criteria (D): Do I understand what I have learnt?   127
    Setting learning goals (E): What do I want to learn?   131
    Evaluating learning content (F): Is this worth learning?   135
Self-assessment: The dilemma for teachers   137
Summary   139

CHAPTER 7 The learner and context: Enjoying the edge of incompetence   **141**

Recognising different understandings of learning   143
Keeping an eye on context   144
Context and student role   145
    The goal setter   146
    The self-assessor   148
    The peer teacher   153
    The peer assessor   155
    The collaborator   159
    The adventurer   160
Self-assessment: Awareness of learning   162
The influence of context: The chameleonic effect   164

References   **167**

Dedication

For Eleanor, a teacher who understood learners and their learning

Acknowledgements

There are many people whose contributions to my own learning enabled this book to be written, not least the young people who spent two years talking with me as "the researcher".

Dr Janet Davies and Dr Alison St George, both of Massey University, generously shared their time and wisdom with me as I completed the data gathering and analysis of learning, both inside and outside school, which later became the foundation of the book.

At various times, Massey University and, more recently, Victoria University have provided a precious collegial research environment in which learning is embraced. During a summer school at the University of Gothenburg, Sweden, Professor Ference Marton and colleagues encouraged me to consider new ways in which to portray and theorise the phenomenon of how young people learn. After I completed my doctorate, Professor Andrew Pollard kindly arranged a period of sabbatical leave at Cambridge University, England, during which I was able to further develop my ideas through presentations to faculty, teachers and educational psychologists.

Over many years, my extended family have supported me in spirit, in real time, glide time and across the globe during this journey of investigating, coming to understand and write about young people's learning.

Associate Professor Bronwen Cowie made helpful comments on the first draft of this book. Professor John O'Neill read several drafts of each chapter and insisted that I should always write what I really want to say.

Finally, Bev Webber of the New Zealand Council for Educational Research gave the support, patience and encouragement needed throughout the publication phase to bring the project to completion.

Foreword

Teachers, we know from the steady accumulation of international evidence, matter enormously in improving pupils' learning outcomes. And policy makers often identify with this—after all, teachers are already in the budget, so perhaps they just need to work harder and everything will be OK? However, the strategy that unlocks improvement concerns teachers working *smarter*. In particular, effective teachers understand learning processes just as much as their subject knowledge. In particular, they need to start from where the children are and respect and support their understanding as it develops. These are the reasons why Roseanna Bourke's book is so important.

The Chameleonic Learner focuses on student voice, self-assessment and learning in context. In other words, the book concerns how children make sense of their learning as they both progress in their studies and build meaning in their lives. The themes of the book are both constructive and practical. We are introduced to the concept of personalisation and the role of careful observation in appreciating students' experiences. Informal and out-of-school relationships and influences on learning are highlighted so that the issues are fully contextualised. But the book comes directly back to the setting of the classroom by drawing attention to student conceptions of learning and the role of self-assessment. Although the focus is on the learner, the essential enabling role of the teacher is never far away. In the final chapter, we are introduced to the idea of "enjoying the edge" of understanding or capability, and this is a crucial issue. It is at the edge that new frontiers are approached, new capacities form and new levels of self-belief develop. If learners are to extend their mastery, they need support in this terrain—provision of which, in social, emotional and cognitive forms, is the essential expertise of the good teacher. But learners are, and always will be, in charge of their own understanding and capabilities as they respond to new contexts and challenges with the brilliant adaptive capacity of the chameleon. This deserves appreciation, and Roseanna Bourke's book shows us how.

Andrew Pollard
Professor of Education
Institute of Education, University of London

Preface

No matter what you *do* today, you will learn. And if you were to think of one thing you have learnt this year, and if you were then to think about the context, place and any people who participated, and whether technology, nature, environment, machinery or books were involved, you would ultimately get to this question: How do I know I have learnt?

This book is about learners and their learning, and how they identify and often assess their own learning. Overall, the book asks and attempts to answer two questions, each based on the premise that learning occurs in all contexts, is measured in a few and is celebrated in others:

- How do we understand the phenomenon of learning in theory, practice, policy and over different contexts?
- How do students conceptualise learning and the self-assessment of their learning?

Learning is a phenomenon that defies definition but about which hundreds of theories abound. Some theorists argue that learning, as a concept, does not exist (Neisser, 1982). Others believe learning can only be understood through metaphors (Hager & Halliday, 2006). For children and young people, learning tends to be a phenomenon that creates a myriad of metaphors and imaginings about life. Before they even realise the complexities of this phenomenon, children can describe and discuss what learning, whether in formal or informal contexts and whether within or outside of school, means to them. And they soon understand that only certain forms of learning are assessed, namely those that their teachers can readily capture (measure) as "outcomes". However, outcomes can also be thought of in terms of learners' views of how they learnt a particular outcome. Here, the assessment, and the strategy used to assess the learning, is the learning experience itself.

Self-assessment is one such form of learning, and it is used by learners across contexts, both at and out of school. The everyday and often multiple learning contexts that young people enjoy, such as rollerblading, judo, swimming, ballet, skateboarding, provide them with authentic environments for learning through self-assessment. When self-assessment is not institutionalised, it plays a major role in helping them identify their learning goals and monitor their progress towards achieving them. Learning for students then becomes about them and their lives, and it leads to motivated, engaged learners who ask questions.

This is because young people are interested in their *own* questions about learning and life. Often when they seek answers through their own questions, they learn more than we can even imagine. They, and we, ask questions with the aim of gaining understanding and of knowing something in a different way; by asking questions, we learn. However, the questions that young children ask are not always those that we, as adults, *think* they are asking.

A television advertisement in New Zealand promoting a car depicts a father driving his young son home. The child, with a serious and intent expression, asks, "Dad, where did I come from?" The rest of the car trip shows the father elaborately describing "the facts" to the sound of Dean Martin belting out, "Let me tell ya 'bout the birds and the bees and the flowers and the trees and the moon up above/And a thing called love." We see fireworks flash, water fountains spout and an array of colourful depictions of life. At the end of the advertisement, having completed the journey and the careful explanation, the father parks the car. The child, bright eyed and excited by his new learning, says, "That's so cool, Dad! Jimmy Johnson only comes from Scotland!"

It is not just children who ask questions and then receive answers better suited to different questions. Sometimes we do not know the questions to ask, but we know *why* we are asking them. For example, when I was working some years ago as an educational psychologist, a teacher asked me to give a psychometric test to a young student. She said that the child's father had specifically requested that his daughter be given an IQ test. During my consultation with the father, he told me of his concerns about his daughter's learning and reading progress. He said he had spent time in a medical library reading up about psychometric tests, specifically, the WISC-R tests. He was convinced his daughter needed testing so her educational difficulties could be identified and her learning problem solved. I sensed the father saw the WISC-R test as a solution to a problem unlikely to be identified by his broad-based questions about IQ tests. So when I asked him, "What is it you *really* want to know?" he said, "I simply want to know why my daughter is not learning to read."

This question gave me a starting point for assessing the child and then providing her with an intervention different from that if I had gone the IQ route. Learning to read is a complex and intricate process that is not readily delineated through use of a psychometric test. This provides an overall test score with subscores, but scores are often irrelevant to the day-to-day teaching and learning that occurs in a classroom. I therefore asked the father if I could use another means of addressing his real question. He agreed.

My approach involved working with the teacher and the child within a classroom context to identify the strategies the child was using, to understand how she conceptualised learning and to determine where and how she was "expressing" the difficulty. The teacher and I looked at ways to support her and the child, especially in respect of offering additional strategies to facilitate reading progress. Within weeks, the child was on the road to becoming a reader, and the father never requested the "IQ" magic again. Nor, for that matter, did the teacher.

This assessment and classroom intervention involved working with the child in order to understand learning from *her* point of view. Children do not see the way adults see, nor do they think the way adults think. As Drummond (1993) found in her research in the United Kingdom, we adults assume we know and understand what children are saying, but in reality, we often do not. The work of Piaget (1929, 1979) has largely influenced our understanding of learning, particularly children's learning. For Piaget, the notion that children's thinking at any given age reflects a unique way of interpreting the world was especially important. This thinking, he said, is not inferior to adults' thinking. Rather, it is qualitatively different. It is this qualitative difference in respect of "thinking" that we can explore with young people so as to better understand their learning—and them.

On another occasion, also during the time I was working as an educational psychologist, I was asked to support a young girl who frequently disrupted her class during mathematics lessons in ways that challenged her teacher and prevented her peers from working. A few days later while observing this class during a physical education (PE) session, I was intrigued to see a child sitting in the sun on a bench, dangling her legs and reading a book, not participating in the PE activity but nevertheless appearing reasonably happy. We started to chat; she told me her name and why she was sitting there. I realised this was the child who had been referred to me as a "behavioural problem". She was not participating in PE because her inappropriate behaviour in the mathematics class preceding this lesson had led to her teacher using nonparticipation in PE as a solution for improving the child's behaviour. This child knew what she wanted: by misbehaving in a preceding mathematics class, she could miss her least favoured curriculum area—PE. Her reasoning in this regard showed her understanding of the system, albeit an understanding born of frustration. She had successfully personalised her learning but had marginalised herself from both her teacher and her peers along the way.

Throughout my practice as a psychologist, I encountered example after example of children and young people attempting to be heard, understood and recognised as successful learners, not "outcome robots". This experience led me to further study how students conceptualise learning and self-assessment in a range of contexts. Interviews and observations that explored their views and experiences in both school and out-of-school settings disclosed a startling metaphor of learning. The students conceptualised learning in various ways, but the setting and the context made a difference: students operated differently according to the multiple contexts they experienced. Just like the child who did not enjoy the PE class, they adjusted their behaviour and learning to determine their degree of participation. Metaphorically speaking, these children changed colour—they were not the same child to all teachers, nor the same child in every setting. Many seemed to know this intuitively and chose when, how and where they acted in the way they did.

The "chameleonic learner" metaphor thus arose from my seeing how learners who achieve well in a range of areas and are accomplished in reading the cues of the learning activity and environment can adapt to that setting yet retain a strong sense of self. What became evident to me was that learners with highly tuned self-assessment systems can maximise their learning opportunities in a range of settings and contexts by changing their approaches to learning.

In the study I report in this book, the learners I observed tended to hold more sophisticated conceptions of learning in out-of-school than within-school contexts. Accordingly, for teachers, understanding students' out-of-school learning contexts can provide invaluable sources and opportunities to develop thinking about learning for school-based settings. As we move to identify personalised learning experiences and opportunities for young people, our essential focus has to be on the learners and their motivation for that learning. To understand how to support this learning, we need to know the right questions to ask our students so that we can understand them as learners. Such questions as "Tell me something you have learnt?" and "How did you know that you had learnt it, and when?" are good starting points.

This book and the study it documents are driven by the belief that "children have much to teach us, if we but stop and listen" (Paley, 1979, p. 142). In writing this book, I wanted not only to validate student experiences in learning but also to acknowledge that even when students do not "appear" to be learning, they most often are. More specifically, my aim has been to explore—through theory, research and student voice—student learning and how this learning is assessed.

Valid expressions of learning enable young people to build their identity and capacity to learn, which is why I foreground, in this book, students' comments (voice) on what learning means to them, and how they know when they have learnt (self-assessment). In recognising student learning, we cannot help but recognise the teachers who support students to know learning in its many guises. Teachers may find it useful to read about these experiences in order to recognise and identify different ways of thinking about learning in classrooms. Learning is, after all, changing the way we think.

The study that I report in these pages follows on from several key studies on student learning. The studies involving children mostly drew on phenomenographic and ethnographic research methodologies. Both are ways of studying and understanding what learning means from the learner's perspective. A phenomenographic approach sets out to present a formal description and understanding of how people experience phenomena (Marton, 1981, 1988; Marton & Booth, 1997). An ethnographic approach seeks to identify the contexts within which these phenomena occur (Lave, 1996; Rogoff, 2003). Finally, while I include, in this book, national and international literature in the area, the voices of the young people in regard to how they conceptualise learning and self-assessment are from New Zealand.

CHAPTER 1

The colour of learning: Why student voice is essential to personalising learning

> If you were a pardalis chameleon, you could change the colour of your skin. In just seconds, you could turn a white coat into a yellow one, decorate yourself with blue stripes, or make dozens of little orange polka dots appear and disappear. You could create all the colours in the rainbow, but you'd probably want to be green. (Darling, 1997, p. 7)

In this first chapter, I present an overview of the content of the book by introducing the notion of personalised learning, explaining why it is important to think about learning and assessment together and why student voice is important to understanding learning. I begin by discussing the chameleon metaphor because this encapsulates one of the key messages of this book: learners view learning in different ways, and adapt to each context according to their motivations to learn, to self-assess, to socialise and to have fun.

Changing colour through learning

The notion that chameleons change the colour of their skin effortlessly and creatively presents an appealing image—but it is not true. Chameleons do change colour, but not as cleverly as is depicted in the many children's books that use chameleons as characters (Mattison, 1989). Nevertheless, the capacity to change colour is the most identifiable feature of a chameleon. For me, using this ability as a metaphor for learning offers an evocative way of describing how learners change and adapt their approaches to learning according to each context while simultaneously retaining a strong sense of self. In other words, learners create their own opportunities to learn when they know their goals, what they need to do to achieve these and what their tools for learning are.

By the time young people reach secondary school, they will, assuming prior successful schooling experiences, have developed a strong sense of self, an identity as a learner and an ability to self-assess their learning across contexts, both within school and out of school. They will know that learning is an integral part of living—that we make choices about how we live and how we learn. Critically, then, "our preferred metaphors and conceptions about learning reflect how we want to live" (Hager & Halliday, 2006, p. 249). Learning thus becomes a personal "aspiration" to know about, to do and/or to understand something, and this aspiration continues throughout life. When we want something badly enough, we apply ourselves to an activity with effort, discipline and determination; we make the learning our own. This process, often referred to in policy terms as the "engaged learner", is, for students, simply about understanding themselves and their own learning needs. In this book, young people talk about how they conceptualise learning, and what self-assessment means for them as a learning tool to support and capture their aspirations.

Because individual aspirations and motivation for learning are both developmentally and socially situated, they are evident at every stage of a child's awareness, whether that involves finding his or her nose as a four-month-old baby, painting visual images of long-legged, spiny-armed people with big faces and happy mouths as a four-year-old, learning to write ideas on paper as a six-year-old or exploring electrical circuits as an 11-year-old. At each stage, young people learn about themselves, about others and about their relationship with the world. They learn to "self-assess" and manage themselves within multiple learning contexts, a process that enables them to form an identity as a learner long before self-assessment becomes an institutionalised process within a school-based setting.

For young people, operating in both formal school-based settings and out-of-school contexts, learning brings ambiguity, hope and contradictions. For some, learning is amorphous; for others, it is outcomes focused. Learning can be fun, exhilarating even, and at other times boring, tedious. It is quantifiable when measured, yet remains immeasurable in many instances. The importance of context is reflected in the numerous and diverse opportunities learners have to explore what learning means to them in different settings with different peers and adults. Context also highlights the fact that each learner is not the same in every setting and that not every setting produces the same learner. The means by which each learner adapts to each context is self-assessment. In order to fully engage with and make the most of each learning activity within any one context, learners rely on being chameleonic learners.

Chameleons change colour to adapt to changing environments and to communicate states such as anger, fear, calm and distress. A green chameleon is peaceful, calm and serene; a yellow chameleon signals surrender. Baby chameleons take a year to learn the language of colours and to read the messages portrayed by these colours through interaction with more mature chameleons (Darling, 1997). Like chameleons, children learn the language of their culture, and they learn to adapt to changing environments. Findings from my two-year study indicate that, while students have different experiences of learning, they interpret each cultural situation through their interactions with teachers, peers and the setting, and they respond differently according to the different contexts. In effect, it is this differentiated response that typifies the chameleonic learner—the learner holds true to his or her identity, but the context for learning influences the "colour" of that learning and the learner's assessment behaviour.

Most young learners need to become adept members of multiple learning cultures and communities (including face-to-face and online social networking). Therefore, the ability to respond to and embrace different cultural contexts is an important aspect of learning because it allows the learner to participate with others in a community of learning—a participation that changes both the individual and others.

Learning, by its nature, is a change process. And "learning, wherever it occurs, is an aspect of changing participation in changing practices" (Lave, 1996, p. 161). In this view, where learning is perceived as participation with others in cultural practices, research shows that individuals employ practices that vary according to distinct circumstances (Rogoff, Moore, Najafi, Dexter, Correa-Chávez, & Solis, 2007). If we are serious about understanding how and why students learn, and if we want to encourage students to learn and self-assess across multiple contexts, thereby enabling them to engage with and actively participate in their learning, then we need to foreground students as learners—to understand how each of them personalises their learning to suit different contexts. And to do this, we need to go beyond merely observing learner behaviour; we need to listen to and hear what students have to say about how they learn. We need to take heed of their voices.

This book is for teachers and teacher educators who already inherently "know" many of the students in this book. Drawing on prevalent theories, research and international policy agendas on student learning, I attempt to make sense of how and why learners experience learning and assessment. For teachers, policy agendas impact on their practice, at times creating their own contradictions and tensions. However, more directly perhaps, students also influence teachers. For teachers, the day-to-day realities of teaching students are often juxtaposed against policies premised on an ideal classroom. By legitimising the student voice, and hearing from these students how learning is neither linear nor static, nor confined to the classroom, teachers can help students better read the policy and social contexts that simultaneously enable and disable learning for both teacher and student.

The personalised learning agenda: Its genesis and relevance

In the United Kingdom, the report of the Teaching and Learning in 2020 Review Group (Department for Education and Skills, 2006) argued that "personalising learning and teaching means taking a highly structured and responsive approach to each child's and young person's learning, in order that all are able to progress, achieve and participate. It means strengthening the link between learning and teaching by engaging pupils—and their parents—as *partners in learning*" (p. 6, emphasis added). In New Zealand, in 2008, the Labour Government introduced an initiative to support learners in senior secondary schools to "become partners" in their learning in order to give them the ability to engage in and direct their own learning beyond school. The Schools Plus policy, since replaced by the National Government's Youth Guarantee policy, addressed the Ministry of Education's concern that a high proportion of students were leaving formal education with few or no formal qualifications. Schools Plus was initiated in response to an acknowledgement that "the system needs to do much more to support young people to stay at school, get good qualifications, and participate in training, education, and employment that sets them up for a positive future" (Ministry of Education, 2008, p. 9).

These developments appear to be working in respect of the twinned aims of personalising learning for students and making students partners in their learning. In its evaluation of the Ministry of Education project Creating Pathways and Building Lives, aimed at "building a sustainable, integrated school-wide approach to career education in 100 secondary schools selected by the Ministry", the Education Review Office[1] (2009) reported evidence of "a more personalised approach as teachers have more awareness of the needs of individual students".

Initiatives such as these reflect the relatively recent international policy agenda of personalising learning. This agenda arose, in part, from a report published by the Organisation for Economic Co-operation and Development (OECD) (2006). The authors of the report observed that "a persistently large share of young people do not complete secondary school, today's baseline for successful entry into the labour market" (OECD, 2006). They argued that low student engagement leads to a drain on countries' economies, presenting an issue not just for governments but also for the young people who make choices that exclude them from a school-based education. These students see an inconsistency between their own aspirations or beliefs in themselves and either the type of learning opportunities open to them in a school-based setting or their understanding of why and how they need to learn in these settings.

---

1 The Education Review Office (ERO) is a government agency that reviews schools and early childhood centres, and reports publicly on the quality of education received by students.

In New Zealand, this situation is evident in the high proportion of students who leave school early, without formal qualifications. When students can legitimately choose to leave school at age 16, they do so in droves. In 2006, of 98,442 full-time students aged 16 and over, 56,895 students (58 percent of the cohort) left school. Only 36 percent of the students who left had a qualification entitling them to entrance to university. There is a strong association between a student's socioeconomic status (SES) and their school exit qualifications. Sixty-four percent of school leavers from decile 10 schools left with a university entrance qualification; only 14 percent of school leavers from decile 1 schools did so.[2]

When the Ministry of Education put in place a strategy to halt the march of 15-year-olds leaving school, in just one year (2006–7), early leaving exemptions halved (Ministry of Education, 2008). The rate of stand-downs and suspensions also dropped. But even so, students from deciles 1 and 2 schools were nearly five times more likely to be suspended from schools than were students in the higher decile schools. Most stand-downs involved students aged 13 to 15, the same age group choosing to leave school, through early leaving exemptions, before the legal age. These students belong to the same demographic of learners contributing to the so-called "long tail" of underachievement described more fully in Chapter 5 and highlighted in multinational studies of student achievement, such as the OECD's Programme for International Student Assessment (PISA).

Personalised learning or just plain learning?

Logically, we can assume that getting students back into learning and raising achievement standards leads to a more educated workforce, thus supporting the "knowledge economy". The economic reward for having a participatory, innovative workforce is considered good for any country, but realisation of this aim relies on young people pursuing learning within the school context—and wanting to do so. And so the ideology of personalised learning was born. This was created in part to address a growing diversity of learning needs, and in part to ensure all young people learn, achieve and ultimately contribute to the economy.

---

2 Decile 10 schools are those schools with the lowest proportion of students from low SES backgrounds. Decile 1 schools have the highest proportion of such students.

In this view, higher standards in education are achieved through more explicit and direct involvement of students as partners in the learning process. Personalised learning works from the expectation that young people can achieve *if* opportunities are created and maximised for them, and *if* that expectation acknowledges the individuality of the child within the social context of the learning.

But what does all this mean for a teacher, faced with an educational landscape in which personalised learning and personal education plans have been added to an ever-changing policy agenda? Are these the latest trends or simply a repackaging of what we already know about learning, and what learning theorists have proposed for centuries? We know learning is conceptualised in different ways according to context, culture and the individual's interests, that socioeconomic status influences learning and that young people's respective cultural capital contributes to how they learn.

Of course, children and young people have always been involved in their own learning, and the very nature of learning means they need to be immersed in the process. What is brought to the fore when learning ideology is personalised is that the role of the learner is explicitly identified in decisions about what is to be learnt, assessed and acknowledged as important. As such, the politics of learning also belongs to the learner.

Personalised learning is described in the United Kingdom's *2020 Vision* report (Department for Education and Skills, 2006) as learner centred, knowledge centred and assessment centred. The report also identifies the specific skills that teachers need in order to personalise their students' learning. These include ability to analyse and use data, to understand learning, to bring about collaborations in the classroom and to support learners to be "active participants in learning" (p. 31). Articulation of these skills leads to an important starting point for teachers trying to comprehend personalised learning—that of gaining understanding of how students conceptualise, and actively participate in, the learning and self-assessment process.

Learning is not a simple concept that we can readily capture through a single theory. Opening up our understanding of the phenomenon of learning requires us to explore the multiple ways learning is described and theorised, and therefore given meaning. Across the range of theoretical positions, "learning" and "the learner" are positioned in different relationships to others and the environment, thereby influencing subsequent decisions about the ways we measure learning or make it visible. Another variable in understanding learning is seen in the prevailing assessment agendas that bring compromise, contradiction and uncertainty to why and how we assess student learning. Since the late 1990s, the assessment agenda relative to learning has increasingly focused on formative assessment—assessment *of* learning, assessment *for* learning and assessment *as* learning. In this book, I accordingly, in an effort to promote understanding of learning, consider formative assessment with reference to self-assessment.

Observing the chameleonic learner: Ways to explore learning through student voice

To understand learning is to understand the learner, and vice versa. Educational researchers systematically engage students in research to understand learning as well as to involve them in an educational reform agenda (Smyth, 2007; Thiessen & Cook-Sather, 2007), and in many cases they attempt to capture the student's view of an experience rather than an adult's interpretation of it (e.g., Rudduck & McIntyre, 2007). But seeing a situation from the student's perspective is rarely easy. Bullough (2007), for example, when striving to draw meaning from the description that Ali, a 12-year-old recent immigrant from Afghanistan, gives of becoming a student in an American school context, observes how difficult it is "to situate Ali in a very few words without doing injustice to the culture or the child" (p. 494). Ali's grandfather and father had been killed by insurgents, he spoke no English and he was struggling to make sense of schooling in a new country. Bullough's story vividly portrays the difficulty all teachers have in truly understanding a culture and the child within it, or the child and the culture within that child, and then bringing that understanding to how and why that child learns. But these challenges can, I believe, be met, if we actively acknowledge that understanding learning from the student's perspective means seeing learning in a different way.

The range of approaches that teachers can take to investigate and describe student learning aligns closely with their teaching approaches and repertoire. Observation, listening and interviewing all provide ways of exploring learning and self-assessment (see Chapter 2). Every classroom is a site for teacher inquiry (or research), and every day-to-day interaction with learners and their learning is an opportunity for teachers to learn. To understand learning is to understand the learner, and to do this teachers need to ask questions, of themselves and of their students.

Teachers who can simultaneously articulate a theoretical position and ask questions in order to understand their students and their learning are at the cusp of teacher inquiry-based practitioner research. By taking this practice further—by talking and writing about their work in order to make their ideas public and open to scrutiny—teachers increasingly are participating in a broader research- and inquiry-led educational community (Loughran, 2002; Loughran & Northfield, 1996). We have much to learn from teachers within classrooms, and the stories they tell about student learning.

Linking theories of learning to "everyday" learning

As part of our journey towards understanding young children and their learning, we need to learn about learning theories so that we can articulate and understand how the acts of teaching and learning are influenced by what we *think* learning is. In Chapter 3, I explore the phenomenon of learning in its many theoretical guises, showing how these influence the way teachers and learners relate to each other.

More importantly, these theories help explain why we do the things we do relative to learning, and not just in a classroom setting but beyond. Consider, for example, teaching young children to rollerblade. Usually, we will do this in a relatively safe setting, where the excited child, rollerblades fitted, can feel and see their own progress. Now consider teaching a reluctant adolescent how to use the washing machine, or indeed where the laundry *is* in the house. The *way* the rollerblading child and the washing-averse adolescent do their respective tasks will depend on whether they perceive the task as positive, and so a learning experience, or whether they see it as a "boring" event in which "learning" is not understood to be taking place. Where learning is concerned, perspective is all, which is why we need to hear students' views on the matter.

Other factors such as context, people, artefacts, tools, technologies and place make a difference to what and how people learn. The sociocultural theories of learning address these specifically, identifying that the "mind" is social and that the development of "identity" is integral to learning. Increasingly, new technologies are bringing learning out of the classroom and into the wider social realm by removing the bricks and replacing them with bytes. In her account of using technology to extend learning opportunities to outside the classroom, Stevenson (2008) describes students being able to personalise their learning through the Web 2.0 environment. Here, they can link up with "experts" able to support that learning. According to Stevenson, this approach provides learners with a powerful means of realising (and self-assessing) their own goals for learning.

In addition to developing and adhering to the various philosophical and theoretical positions on learning, researchers have explored the effects of learning on students in an attempt to capture the multiplicities of the phenomenon that is learning. While some educational researchers describe learning as deep, surface and strategic (Entwistle, 1987; Marton & Säljö, 1976), and distinguish between ontological learning and epistemological learning (Packer & Goicoechea, 2000), there is general agreement amongst those interested in this field that learning is social and is about "change". It not only evolves over the long term, but is also a minute-by-minute process of grappling with the known and unknown: "we are constantly and inevitably changing, even if in small ways, becoming different types of people as we learn new things" (Wortham, 2006, p. 25).

Students' conceptions of learning

As I note in Chapter 3, Plato considered knowledge an innate construct and that learning therefore is about understanding ourselves and our knowledge within. Other philosophers, however, took the position that we are born with an "empty slate". Young learners, not having heard of these theories, and not often asked to describe their learning theories, or their conceptions of learning, can nevertheless articulate ways to think about learning.

And this they do, very clearly, in Chapter 4. Here, students describe and discuss what learning means to them. Their diverse views reflect a range of theoretical positions, from "I need to fill up my brain" to "I was born with everything I know." Two different views from learners show how students' conceptions of learning are important for two reasons. First, the ways students think about learning affect how they approach a learning activity. Second, and irrespective of the view that a teacher may have about learning, it is what the student thinks they are "supposed to do" that drives their work. Bridging this gap becomes enabling for both teacher and learner (Boulton-Lewis, Marton, Lewis, & Wilss, 2000; Marton, 1981).

The students' conceptions of learning outlined in this book derive from the results of my study involving Years 7 and 8 students (11- to 12-year-olds). Because children's learning is not school bound or confined to specific, formal learning events, I wanted to explore the varied and changing ways they learn, and how they themselves describe that learning, during both in-school and out-of-school settings. Analysis of the students' commentary led me to develop five categories of description, ranging in scope from views that learning is about acquiring knowledge and is accessed through external means, to views that learning is about "seeing" or understanding "differently".

Assessment agendas

In his classroom-based research, Wortham (2006) showed that in a school context, and specifically a classroom setting, academic learning and nonacademic learning are inextricably linked. As such, nonacademic factors such as power relations, interpersonal struggles and identity are entwined in determining how students engage with academic material content such as reading, science and mathematics. This consideration raises the question of what we actually measure when we assess student learning.

Much of this book is based on the premise that "assessment, rather than teaching, has a major influence on students' learning. It directs attention to what is important" (Boud & Falchikov, 2007, p. 3). And of key interest with regard to student learning is the question, important for whom? In Chapter 5, I outline assessment issues in relation to teaching, drawing out, in particular, the tension that teachers tend to experience when trying to reconcile assessment for accountability with assessment for learning; neither of which addresses an agenda for assessment to *understand* learning.

Given the number and complexity of learning theories, it is not surprising that measurement of learning is highly contentious. If the *process* of learning is difficult to define, *measurement* of that learning becomes even more tangled and complex. What exactly are we measuring through our chosen assessments of student learning, and what does this tell us about our own views of learning or about our beliefs of what can be reliably and validly measured? For many educators, concern mounts that because we are not enabling students to learn and to self-assess beyond the formal assessment systems they encounter, we are failing to prepare them for lifelong learning, to make choices about their employment beyond school and to exercise sound judgement during their careers (Tan, 2007).

Three specific issues relating to assessment are relevant to this discussion. First, assessment practices do not reflect the different theoretical positions of learning. Second, we tend, especially in school settings, not to measure actual learning but rather the product or outcome of that learning. And third, the dominant focus on assessment strategies since the late 1990s—on efficient assessment methods, and specifically on formative assessment for learning strategies—has eclipsed the fundamental point that these assessment practices control how students conceptualise *learning*. This conceptualisation influences the choices that students make about how, when and why they choose to learn or, at times, to disengage from school-based learning.

Students' conceptions of self-assessment

As I discuss in Chapter 6, all of the students in my study were aware of having learnt something and therefore held conceptions of self-assessment similar to their conceptions of learning described in Chapter 4. The students' conceptions of self-assessment ranged from a basic awareness of knowing they had learnt when an external source provided the information, to students who experienced an awareness of learning through their internal knowledge of self with an understanding of the concept they were learning. Students who needed external support to confirm that learning had occurred had little confidence in their own ability to assess their learning. However, students who identified that they relied less on the explicit support of others and more on their own beliefs, expectations and goals for learning held more sophisticated conceptions of self-assessment; they also tended to talk more confidently about their learning.

But even this last group of students recognised the role that others played in supporting their learning and self-assessment. For example, when using both out-of-school and school contexts as the basis from which to discuss learning and self-assessment, students talked about using the support of other people to identify what they should be learning and how to self-assess that learning. They drew on this support in two ways. First, they actively and intentionally used or watched others (adults, siblings and peers) to demonstrate a performance. The students explained that this process, which occurred mainly in out-of-school contexts, allowed them to see from others what the "end product" or outcome, such as batting in cricket, of the learning would look like. Second, they sought out peers and siblings to "translate" difficult or intricate instructions or concepts. For example, when a student had difficulty with a mathematics concept, she enlisted the support of her peers to explain it to her.

When describing self-assessment in out-of-school settings, students seemed more aware both of what they had learnt and of what they needed to learn. This learning was characterised by voluntary participation and choice of activity. Relevance and inherent interest were strong motivating factors, so contributing to the students' high level of engagement with the learning. There was a focus on the *whole* of learning, such as making picture frames, jazz dancing, playing the piano. In contrast, at school, there seemed to be a sense of accessing and assessing learning in isolated units, such as certain spelling words, multiplication tables, writing stories on a theme. For many students, the whole was generally unclear, rendering the intent or point behind the learning ambiguous.

Assessment and learning in context

In Chapter 7, I return to the chameleon metaphor: theories of learning incorporate multiple understandings of learning, and the way students "do" learning reflects this diversity. We see this through the diverse learning roles the students in my study were taking—those of goal setter, self-assessor, peer teacher, peer assessor, collaborator, adventurer. If young people are to flourish in any learning environment, irrespective of its social milieu and assessment system, they need diverse contexts for learning, assessment and cultural activities. The choices that individuals make about their learning determines whether they are successful. The choices depend on their strengths, gifts and talents, and their assessment of that learning on their own terms, in their areas of interest.

Making choices about learning

In his children's story, *The Mixed-Up Chameleon*, Eric Carle (1984) uses a chameleon to explore the desire to be like others, do what others do, be as smart or as handsome as others and live in another's shoes, colour or shape. At the end of the story, having wished for and been granted the characteristics of a fish, a giraffe, an elephant, people and a fox, among many others, the chameleon simply wants to catch a fly. Totally mixed up by his many guises, the chameleon finds this usually natural activity impossible and just wishes to be himself. When this final wish comes true, the chameleon catches the fly—and (presumably) is happy!

In this story, Eric Carle draws on some features of learning that all young children experience, in particular the desire to be like others while retaining the essential sense of self. But, as I point out in this book, unlike the chameleon in Eric Carle's story, children learn tasks, activities and new ways of thinking not merely by wishing to be like others and being able to do what others can do. Children talk about "hard work" in order to capture that sense of achievement brought about by intentional and meaningful learning experiences. Thus, in a successful learning experience, learners experience three integral phases:
- *recognition* and understanding of features and abilities demonstrated by others that they currently are not able to do themselves
- the *desire* to be able to do these
- the *belief* that, ultimately, and with perseverance, they will be able to perform the identified activities.

The last phase, belief, is a necessary component that moves learning beyond the initial intended outcome.

For some children, to "be" an actor, an astronaut, a dancer is about the excitement associated with an activity, a way of life, they imagine they would enjoy. By watching others around them, children identify characteristics that appear desirable, but they have not yet learnt how those characteristics support the essence of them as a learner, nor are they fully aware of how these contribute to their growing sense of identity. This yearning—the wanting to know about something, to do something or to be someone—is an important aspect of learning for young people because it ultimately leads to the purpose they place on a learning activity.

Without innate goal setting, without having something to strive for and without a belief they will get there, learning becomes an arduous, unintentional process of discrete parts set before them. How will learning numbers get you to the moon? How does understanding gravity make you a better dancer? Simple belief in the possibility of "getting there" *as a result of* their learning enables young people to continue to try out new ways of doing things, to explore aspects of engaging in various activities as part of their learning, to understand why they are learning, how they are learning and what they need to do to direct their own learning.

CHAPTER 2

Changing the way we see student learning

> Researchers who seriously engage in the work of seeking out, taking up, and re-presenting students' experiences of school not only translate what they gather but are also translated by it. (Cook-Sather, 2007, p. 829)

Although researchers can spend time with learners, observing and recording and talking and interacting with them, teachers have the unique, first-hand experience of translating their own observations of their students grappling with learning activities. In this chapter, I explore ways teachers can understand learning in the classroom, as well as ways that require a more systematic focus when researching with learners. The question at the heart of this chapter is this: How do we inquire into student learning and translate their experiences of it?

Teacher as researcher

Whether we are teacher or researcher, it is important to realise that both provide different means of considering the phenomenon of learning, and that arguably both are needed to portray a full picture of what it means "to learn". The metaphor of the chameleonic learner requires us to develop an understanding of student learning as "in the moment" and "in this context" (Nuthall, 2007), and constantly negotiated (Dyson, 2007). It also requires us to articulate the relationships between learners, their peers, their teachers and the activity. The focus of research or classroom inquiry by the teacher is thus on *understanding* learning rather than attempting to *change* that learning. If teachers are to change anything within a classroom context, their first step is to listen, watch, gather meaning and really understand what "learning" means *in this context*. Analysing learning and self-assessment in action is always an important aspect of teaching. The process of systematically looking at learning, examining and translating what we see and supporting learners to understand their own learning is the aim of classroom inquiry.

Understanding student learning within a formal educational context involves observations, conversations, careful questioning, constant listening and searching for ways to "see the world" through the mind of the learner. When we participate in a community, we contribute to change and are, in turn, changed by our dynamic interactions with others (Rogoff, 2003); thus, classroom inquiry enables change. By being willing to learn from students, those of us who are teachers and researchers *intentionally* change. If we view learning as something that happens only to students and that is measured by outcomes, then the teacher–learner relationship becomes a one-sided process of pulling students along. In the same way that learning is a process of changing conceptions—that is, changing the way we see things—teacher inquiry is about seeing our classrooms, our students and ourselves in a different way.

Systematic effort to understand learning means ensuring that the process of analysing and interpreting data collected within the classroom is characterised by attention to detail and rigour. Inquiry means uncovering and explaining what is happening. But teachers are not necessarily inclined to theorise or make explicit their interactions with learners. Classroom activities, and the learning within, are rarely public events, and constant verbal and nonverbal interactions with students allow teachers little time to think about, reflect on or write about their work for others to learn from. In contrast, classroom inquiry involves making these experiences public and therefore open to scrutiny. This is an important step in research (Stenhouse, 1981).

The starting point for teachers as classroom inquirers is to identify one aspect of their teaching that interests them and that they believe is pivotal to student learning. Initially, it does not matter whether that aspect is a way of relating, a form of assessment, a communication to parents or a conversation with students. Concentrating on something that interests them *as a teacher* will help bring the learning of students into focus. Significantly, the process will also focus on the teacher as learner.

When, as teachers, we are interested in the impact of the *meanings* of events for students rather than the *effects* of those particular events on students, we give credence to these perspectives:
- Students do their work on the basis of the meaning they give to it (not the meaning given by teachers or others).
- Students figure out what things mean to them by working, talking with and learning from their peers and teachers.
- These interactions adjust and change the way students think about things and their meanings.

Classroom inquiry into student learning must therefore appreciate the influence individuals have on different contexts and groups, as well as the influence these contexts and groups have on the individual.

The notion of "partnership" is essential when undertaking inquiry of this kind because the teacher relies in great part on interviews or structured conversations with the students in order to understand and learn about the focus of inquiry from the students' experiences. In general, if this interview process is approached with sensitivity and care, most students are comfortable about talking. As Eisner (1998) notes, "It is surprising how much people are willing to say to those whom they believe are really willing to listen" (p. 183). Interviews can be an enriching experience for learners, too (Kvale, 1996).

The study in brief

The young people who took part in the study described in this book were in Year 7 and Year 8 at school. During the study, which I conducted in order to better understand how students conceptualise learning and self-assessment, I interviewed

26 students (15 males and 11 females) from three Year 7 classes in one intermediate school, and I involved seven of these students the following year, when they were in Year 8, in an ethnographic phase of study. During the first year, my interviews with the students ranged from 35 to 60 minutes. Interview time depended on the speed of the student's utterances and the amount of information each student wanted to share. During the second year, I observed and interviewed Year 8 students in both school-based and out-of-school contexts. I also analysed relevant documents. I audiotaped and transcribed verbatim all interviews conducted across the two phases of the study.

My analysis of the Year 7 transcripts began with no predetermined framework and involved an iterative process in which I read the transcripts several times, first to identify categories of learning, and second to identify categories of self-assessment. In many cases, I found instances of students talking about learning something and simultaneously explaining how or when they knew they had learnt (an example of self-assessment). I explored these transcripts in terms of the students' conceptions of both learning and self-assessment. The categories of description that I eventually drew out (see Chapters 4 and 6) move from least sophisticated and least inclusive views to most sophisticated and inclusive views, thereby providing hierarchical models for conceptions of both learning and self-assessment.

Discussing learning with students

Interviews, conversations, dialogue and "talking to kids" invariably involves questioning. The careful selection and phrasing of questions can greatly affect what we can learn from students and how we help them think about their own learning. The questions we ask and the way we frame these create different response possibilities, which is why I decided to use a semistructured interview schedule with additional questions generated on the basis of the students' responses. Therefore, while the structure within each interview was predetermined, no two interviews were the same.

I also made careful and systematic use of probe questions to help students clarify, elaborate on or explain their responses. While probe questions do not

necessarily contain much in their structure or content, they are useful because they encourage participants to amplify or clarify their explanations. Examples of probe questions include:
- Would you say something more about ...?
- What do you mean by that?
- Can you give me an example?
- Could you clarify what you mean?

An example of opening up a conversation about learning with a student, young or old, is as simple as asking them what learning is. This is not a closed question, and can involve all curriculum areas. For the child, talking about learning is usually novel, at least in part because they have not thought about or articulated their understanding of it as a phenomenon. They usually have discussions about what they have learnt, what their learning intentions are and what the results of assessment show they have learnt, but not what learning is *for them.*

I began each interview with this question: "When you knew we were going to talk about learning, what did you think we'd talk about?" The children's initial responses located them firmly in a school-bound context. Examples included:
- I thought study, something like that.
- What we liked about the school, what we learn and stuff.
- I don't know, school.
- I wasn't really sure. Subjects and stuff.
- School work, anything to do with learning, like what I do on the average day.
- Finding out things. Researching.
- About what the working environment was like, and what sort of things we learnt in a certain curriculum.
- Spelling and times tables and all that and division.
- What I do when I do maths and reading.
- How you like school and what subject you like, and how the school works.
- Education and stuff.

These typical responses show how students tend *not* to think about learning beyond school-based learning—until, that is, they are prompted later in the conversation with "Does learning happen anywhere else?" But, having taken that school-based thinking as a first step, learners open up their ideas and think about what learning actually *is*.

What do you mean?

Talking with students allows us to continually explore the meaning they attribute to a topic. While students in this study used a common language when talking about learning within school, they often placed different meanings on these ideas. We all use words that explain or elaborate an idea; usually, we know what we mean, and the word itself generates further, multiple layers of meaning encapsulating personal history and context. Take the word "gay", for example. Young people today use this word as an adjective to describe something they do not particularly value or like; they are not referring to a form of gaiety, nor to the sexual orientation of a person. They may exclaim, "That story's so gay," or question your sartorial sense by asking, "Why are you wearing those gay trousers?" In these cases, they respect neither the story nor the trousers; they think they are stupid, dumb, old-fashioned—and here, too, we are using words that have multiple meanings for each person.

When young skateboarders at a skateboarding park were asked about the use of the term "gay", they described it as concealing jealousy while congratulating their peers on stunts. As one of them explained, "If he's doing a trick that I can't do, I'll probably call him gay or something because I can't do it." Said another, "In all honesty, what it is, is like to express a form of *slight* jealousy, but at the same time, you're, like, wow, my friend just did that. That's awesome! It's almost like saying, 'Man, I can't believe you just did that, I wish I could do that.' In all honesty, it's not portrayed as negativity in most scenarios up here" (Petrone, 2010, p. 126).

So, when talking with young people, it is important to constantly check what they mean by their language, because adults often receive messages very different from those intended. We cannot assume that when students refer to learning or assessment, or use the words "boring", "fun", "cool", our understanding of these terms coincides with theirs. The young people in this book often used the word "boring", making it necessary to ask, "When you say *boring*, what do you mean?" For example, one student clarified boring as work that is too hard. Another referred to work considered too mundane and repetitive.

Interestingly, students in a study conducted by Pollard, Broadfoot, Croll, Osborn, and Abbott (1994) were more likely to define boring as "teacher-framed work" and work that involved "doing what the teacher says" (p. 173). The students in Filer's (1997) study used boring in relation to news items presented to the class in a manner that would please the teacher, rather than in a comedic form that would appeal to their peers. Boring was identified in Anthony's (1994) study of secondary school students in a mathematics context as, "the result of the work being too hard or uninteresting" (p. 230). It seems that, in a school context, students who do not always appreciate the point of learning an isolated spelling word or a particular multiplication table tend to refer to learning as boring.

In the study in this book, learners used the words "practice" and "boring" in different ways depending on their conception of learning. For a student with a less sophisticated view of learning, *practice* meant remembering facts for later recall; for a student with a more sophisticated view of learning, practice involved applying the knowledge and skills to a new task. However, these meanings also changed according to context, so for the same learner practice could mean different things. For one learner, practice in trampolining was different from practice in spelling. For those learners with a sophisticated conception of learning, *boring* meant repetitive, arduous tasks undertaken when they already understood a concept; for others, it meant a difficult task that they did not understand. Some students used the term "boring" when they did not see or value the point of the learning. The implication for teachers is the need to discover the learners' understanding of a task or word because it determines the way they approach the task.

Here are some examples of what boring meant to the learners in my study:

Boring is when the activity is compulsory	At school, some of the time it's boring and some of the time it's fun, and whenever you're at home it's always fun because you like doing it because you can just give up on it whenever you like. So if it's boring, you just say, 'I don't want to do this anymore,' and you just give up on it and do something else.
Boring is when there is no perceived relevancy	'Cause, if it's boring, well, you're just writing it out and writing down the answer, and it's boring. And if it's fun, well, you actually get into it and do it properly.
Boring is when the activity is not practical	If you get to do something ... because, like, in maths, you don't get actually something, you just get the knowledge—that's real boring.
Boring is practising a skill or concept you already understand	R: So what do you mean by boring? S: Like, when you just have to do reading and just write out answers for it, when you know that they're all going to be right exactly, and you know everything all right, and you, like, just revision, but it's too much revision when you know what you're doing all the time; it's too much to do and it's too easy. R: Ah, so boring learning is when it's too easy? S: Yeah, really too easy. Really, really, really easy.

We can clarify the *meaning* and *interpretation* students give to concepts by:
1. requesting examples of what the student is saying
2. asking students directly what they mean by certain things
3. creating links between events and settings (such as home and school learning)
4. constantly checking for shared meaning—even if the *words* used are the same. For example, teachers can more easily develop a shared understanding of how to change their teaching when they understand that "boring" for one child means repetitive but for another means too hard
5. exploring a concept in different and multiple ways. For example, when focusing on issues about assessment, we can ask students how they knew *when* and *how*

they had learnt, and whether they knew before the teacher (or parent) that learning had occurred.

Listening for the metaphors

It is very interesting to listen for the metaphors students choose when they talk about their learning. For students, metaphors provide a way of explaining and describing their experiences and understanding when words alone are not enough. Students may refer to tape recorders when discussing memorising information, or clouds when discussing knowledge. Dall'Alba (1994) said that students in her study "used rich metaphors to capture their understanding of what learning is" (p. 79). Teachers can use these metaphors to help students clarify ideas and explain complex issues. Among the metaphors the young learners in my study used were these:

> *Your mind's like **a tape recorder**, like, that we're on now, and it just takes in the information and you don't even really know you've got it. That's how I find it ... You're mostly recording something all the time because, like, I'll remember talking to you now, so I've basically recorded it because I've remembered I've been talking to you.*
>
> *Knowledge is like **a cloud, a bubble**, you don't even know what it is ... I think you always have a knowledge when you were born to do stuff ... I think you always have it there, and then when you're told it, you're kind of, you take it in and then remember it, and then you might let it out, but you always keep it there.*
>
> *It's like a file, **one of those file cabinets**, and you, like, you just pull it out of your mind like a file cabinet, and you pull something out ...*
>
> *[R: If you can't pull it out?]*
>
> *That means you haven't learnt it.*

Observing in the classroom

Effective teachers are keen and constant observers. Usually, they see the make-up of the milieu as it unfolds in front of them in multidimensional mode. They keep track of the learner reading in front of them, the group activity to the side, the students working independently, the child running his ruler alongside the windowpane and listening to the sound, the child with her fingers in her pencil case scrabbling for her pencil. Another student ambles by and asks a question; meanwhile, the teacher notes the two children seated side by side at the computer. Scanning the periphery, seeing the learning activity around the classroom, is what a teacher constantly does.

Part of the nature of this observation involves parallel analysis of what is going on—knowing when to intervene, remain silent, glare, smile in encouragement, show mock horror, ask questions, make comments, tell a joke. Observations thus require some form of analysis that leads to a chosen form of action. It is the analysis component of the observation that translates the "seen" and "scene" activity to a teaching activity, and progressively to a research or inquiry approach. For example, a teacher may see an activity in action, say, a group of young children gathered around a desk examining a reading book. But unless that teacher does some measure of analysis (even subconsciously) of what, how, when and where learning is occurring for these children, then teaching is less likely to take place.

While a teacher's analysis of everyday observations in a classroom is not always transparent, it nevertheless marks the difference between (a) a quick scan around the room to check students are on task and (b) active teaching. Teachers' informed decisions and judgements about their day-to-day teaching, often derived from observational data, draw on a range of strategies including memory, interpretation, learning theory and motivation theory:

- *Memory*: Teachers cannot remember every interaction and event that occurs in a classroom. Usually what they recall are those events that had a strong emotional effect on them or that fell outside their regular classroom routine. A teacher might recall the day the child overturned a desk but not the book that made the child upset. The teacher might recall feeling elated when Martin finally grasped complex equations but not remember the earlier occasion when he understood fractions, something he was very excited about. Because, during an analysis, ability to recall events, days, times and people is important, keeping a daily diary over a short period (e.g., a month) will help teachers track what actually happened.

- *Interpretation*: When teachers recall an event and situation, they view it through the lens of their interpretation and understanding; they derive particular meaning from what they observe and remember. Teachers thus remember less about the activity and more about the meaning they give to the event. In many cases, this interpretation remains the teacher's view and does not capture the learner's intention or reason for her behaviour. Consequently, if the interpretation is to faithfully represent the learning, the teacher needs to consider the meaning behind the child's intent and the context in which the child engaged in the activity.
- *Learning theory:* All teachers theorise their teaching and learning, but often subconsciously. They may make decisions and judgements about what is happening according to what they think "learning" is. Analysis helps teachers reflect on their learning theories and determine whether their own interpretation includes other ways of seeing learning. On what basis is their judgement sound? Should they challenge that judgement?
- *Motivation theory:* In general, children do want to learn, succeed and feel good about themselves. They want to learn and to live. In official discourse, this desire is often referred to as being "engaged" in learning. Student engagement is not an issue if children love to learn, feel secure in their learning environment and enjoy the challenge of the unknown. Teachers analysing an event from the perspective of motivation need to ask these sorts of question:
    - "Why did Joe choose to do this?"
    - "How can I support Joe to be more energetic in his work?"
    - "Does Joe view this work as relevant and what parts does he value?"

Observing outside the classroom

Realistically, teachers can observe only a small part of what, how and when young people learn outside the classroom. When observing young people in their school-based out-of-classroom contexts (the hall, drama room, fields, netball courts, playground and so on), we see how different social and learning settings influence the students' interactions with others and contribute to their growth of self-awareness and identity. Subsequently, our understanding of these students is far greater. The student a teacher sees in mathematics is not the same student when participating in sport. The student may be seen as competitive and tenacious in one context and a struggling learner in another. Students do not generally know to look at their learning of abseiling and to use these principles in science, *yet they are the same learner.*

Out-of-school settings influence how young people learn and they also influence how young people think about learning. To develop an inclusive understanding of learning, we need to explore these out-of-classroom and out-of-school contexts with the learners. When it is not possible to observe learners in multiple contexts, questions can help:

- "Can you tell me where else you learn?"
- "Can you tell me something you have learnt out of school this year?"
- "How did you know when you had learnt it?"

Learners' responses to and interactions with environments outside and within formal contexts differ. The most interesting part of observing learners in out-of-classroom contexts is seeing what cues they respond to, and why. Several factors affect their decisions, including their personal goals and motivation, their peer group, the level of adult participation (teacher, parent, instructor) and the context within which the activity is framed. Students learning to count to 10 in Japanese learn differently in a classroom context in which the aim is to learn Japanese as a language, compared to a judo context where learning to count to 10 in Japanese is part of a routine.

Bringing to the fore what is to be analysed

Each classroom is a rich, diverse, lively environment in which to observe learning. We can choose to observe the whole or parts of that whole. For example, we can observe individual learning and focus on one or two learners, or we can observe pairs or clusters of learners or we can take a whole-class view. The metaphorical lens we use to observe in an educational context is shaped by our understanding and theoretical position of learning and what we highlight in our observations; hence creating a picture of learning *at that moment*. What is brought to the fore and what we choose to place in the background make a difference. Thus, while the general context remains an integral part of the activity, it is what we focus on or highlight that is of interest. Our choice depends on the focus of the classroom inquiry.

Summary

In this chapter, I outlined some of the ways teachers can begin to explore and understand student learning rather than merely "measure" it. Teachers who understand learning—and learners—can help their students make sense of what they are doing and why. In order to understand student learning, teachers need to be multiskilled in observing, listening, questioning, interpreting, analysing and articulating what they see. This work is complex and intricate when positioned alongside teaching, but for many teachers this *is* teaching. Teacher inquiry is more like research activities than many teachers realise. By adjusting some components of what they already do, teachers can easily embark on systematic inquiry into student learning. The next chapter provides a theoretical framework on learning and provides a context that leads into the students' conceptions of learning presented in Chapter 4.

CHAPTER 3

Learning: It's what we do

"You'd better stay a long time."
"Excuse me?"
"You'd better stay a long time if you want to learn something about us or drama or school." (Gallagher & Lortie, 2007, p. 405)

The young person in Gallagher and Lortie's study puts up a challenge for teachers and researchers: be with students for the long haul to understand them and their learning. From an early age, children form beliefs, conceptions and ideas about school and learning. Through participation in increasingly formal education settings, often starting with a formative early childhood experience, children develop their ideas and beliefs about what "learning" is and how they need "to learn". These have been called "folk learning theories" (James, 2008; Lampert, Rittenhouse, & Crumbaugh, 1996)—theories that we create to understand why we do what we do in different learning settings.

While *being* with learners is part of getting to know and understand them and the phenomenon of learning, so too is understanding the theoretical views that position learning in different ways. To really understand learners, we need not only to appreciate these different views of learning but also to clarify our own such views of learning. In this chapter, I consider relevant theoretical views on learning, at all times keeping in mind the question, *What is learning?*

Theoretical understandings of learning

Theorists position learning and the learner in different ways, and the fact that they do demonstrates how knowledge and how we come to know "something" are variously understood and valued. Although theorists—and teachers—hold different beliefs and assumptions about what learning is, we need to consider multiple ways of thinking about *learning* because doing so helps us understand how people learn and, more specifically within the context of this book, enables teachers to talk with young learners about their own learning.

Many learning theories have developed over the centuries to explain this elusive phenomenon. Brief descriptions of the ways theorists have attempted to explain and research learning follow.

Classical theory

The classical theory of learning, attributed to Plato (427–347BC), suggests all knowledge is innate and that learning is merely a process of recalling this reality. Plato (*The Republic*) explains this theory in a story featuring a young warrior, Er, who is taken for dead on a battlefield but wakes 12 days later. He describes how his soul departed from him, as did the souls of his dead comrades. The souls have their futures determined. They get to choose what they want to "be", and their decisions are based on their experience of the life they each have already lived. All the souls are told to drink from the river of Forgetfulness. As they drink, they forget everything about this experience, and they also forget the knowledge they acquired before being reborn. Some drink more than their measure. That they do explains why some people have difficulty learning—they have "forgotten" too much of their previous knowledge to recall. However, Er is forbidden to drink from the water, so he retains his memory of the experience and is able to relay the story when he wakes from his coma. For Plato, learning was the process of recalling what the soul had already seen and absorbed.

The philosopher Locke (1653–1704) similarly believed the ability to learn is innate and that the faculties we are born with determine our learning. However, in contrast to Plato, Locke argued that the mind is "white paper void of all characters, without any *ideas*" (Locke, 1977, p. 33). Both Plato and Locke took the view that learning is individualistic, but Locke also argued that knowledge itself is innate. His theory was based on the position that infants come into the world with a mind devoid of content and that learning takes place as a result of certain biologically determined abilities. Both these views present the learner as a passive being, especially during the stages of knowledge acquisition.

For some learners, the classical view represents how they understand learning. An 11-year-old girl in my study exemplified this when, after she had said learning is about "taking in knowledge", I asked her to describe what she meant by this:

> R: *Where was it in the first place, before you took it in, where was this knowledge?*
> S: *I think it's actually quite a strange question, because I have to actually guess, I think that it actually all it ... I think just before I was born, I think that it was actually all in there, but everything I was going to learn was already in there, but I had to actually experience and have it told to me, learn it, and I think it was, I think some of it I learnt when I was quite young, and I still use it now and, like, different ways to draw and different ways to paint and ...*
> R: *So you're saying you were born with this knowledge?*
> S: *Yeah. I think you were born with the special knowledge that you ... I think you're actually born with a special knowledge of how to crawl and how to sit, how to actually eat. I think you were born with that, that you actually understand it all then. Because when you think about it, you actually, knowledge is like a cloud, a bubble, you don't even know what it is, it's just like words that you just take in later on. I think you always have a knowledge when you were born to do stuff that some kids can't do, and so I think you always have it there, and then when you're told it you're kind of, you take it in and then remember it, and then you might let it out but you always keep it there.*

Behavioural theories

Two theories dominated throughout the behavioural period and continue to influence behavioural theories. These were the classical conditioning theory of Ivan Pavlov (1849–1936) and the operant conditioning theory of E. L. Thorndike

(1874–1949). Both theories began with a look at how animals react, as a means of survival, to their environments. The two theorists then used this information to describe how people react to their environments. While Pavlov was interested in stimulus and how it could be manipulated to seek a response, Thorndike concentrated on the response itself; he was interested in how a response altered or manipulated the behaviour of animals and, later, people.

B. F. Skinner developed this theory further in the late 1930s by showing that random rewards are more effective than frequent or systematic rewards in altering a person's behavioural pattern (Skinner, 1972). Skinner's theory was based in part on the assumption that "almost all living things act to free themselves from harmful contacts" (p. 26); therefore, behaviour can be shaped through negative reinforcement. The similarities and underlying assumptions of these theories within the behavioural paradigm are that behaviour can be *shaped* and that learning is simply the acquisition of a new behaviour. There is no reference to the mental or cognitive acts informing that acquisition.

Cognitive theories

As a reaction against what was perceived to be a mechanistic and reductionist approach to learning with minimal emphasis on cognitive considerations, theorists began to move away from describing learning as only that which could be observed. This shift represented a change in thinking, from learning that could be broken down into discrete tasks and studied in detail to a holistic approach where learning is viewed as a continuous, complex process.

The work of Piaget (1929, 1979), in particular, strongly influenced understanding of learning, by contributing to the knowledge that children's thinking at any given age reflects a unique way of interpreting the world. For instance, whether the learner is 5, 12 or 16 years old, there are qualitative differences in what and how they know. Piaget developed the notion that learners are not passive individuals waiting to be shaped and moulded by environmental pressures, but are intentional learners who act on their environment.

Piaget's work recognised that the social world has an impact on the individual's development insofar as the individual adapts to the environment (Piaget, 1929, 1979).

Although Piaget's work examined the individual's development across contexts, in general, Rogoff, Mistry, Göncü, and Mosier (1993) argued that his work did not take into account the complex social environment in which the child learns. Their argument was that the primary focus of Piaget's work "was on the individual rather than on the aspects of the world that the child struggles to understand or on how the social world contributes to individual development" (p. 5).

Sociocultural theory

The arguments put forward by Rogoff and her colleagues drew on sociocultural theory, which focuses on the social world of learning, and how context contributes to a child's development. Based on Lev Vygotsky's theory of learning and development, sociocultural theory has influenced much of the contemporary research on learning.

Vygotsky developed his thinking by first identifying three extant theoretical positions in relation to development and learning:

1. *Processes of child development are independent of learning:* Adherents of this position argue that learning is an external process not actively involved in development. Development is always a prerequisite for learning, and if a child's mental functions (intellectual operations) have not matured to the extent that he or she is capable of learning a particular subject, then no amount of instruction or teaching will prove useful.
2. *Learning is development:* According to followers of this position, learning and development occur simultaneously; they coincide, in the same way that two identical geometrical figures coincide when superimposed.
3. *Learning involves a combination of the above two theoretical positions:* The proposal here is that the process of maturation prepares and makes possible a specific process of learning, and this, in turn, stimulates and pushes forward the maturation process. Therefore, learning and development occur simultaneously as a result of their impact on each other.

Vygotsky argued that these positions are not useful for examining the relational view of learning and development, where learning precedes development. He accordingly developed a theory based on what he termed the *zone of proximal development* (ZPD). The ZPD, which is "the distance between the actual developmental level as determined by independent problem-solving and the level of potential development as determined through problem-solving under adult guidance or in collaboration with more capable peers" (Vygotsky, 1978, p. 86), emphasises the importance of social contexts for intellectual achievements.

Moll and Whitmore (1993) note that Vygotsky used this concept "to emphasise the importance—in fact the inseparability—of sociocultural conditions for understanding thinking and its development" (p. 19); this development is thus the difference between some measure of independent achievement and some measure of guided achievement. This thinking led to Vygotsky's theoretical position being interpreted in the sense of "personal achievement is always within a collective approach ... [which means that Vygotsky] denies the reality of independent achievement itself" (Morss, 1996, p. 22). However, Vygotsky argued that we go through a process in which we socially construct an external activity before constructing it internally, thereby articulating his recognition of an internal—or individual—reality: "every function in the child's cultural development appears twice: first, on the social level, and later, on the individual level; first, *between* people (*interpsychological*), and then *inside* the child (*intrapsychological*). All the higher functions originate as actual relations between human individuals" (Vygotsky, 1978, p. 57).

The implication of Vygotsky's work for teachers centres on two key ideas: (1) that other people (teacher, parent, peers) are central to mediating both learning and assessment processes, and (2) that learning is not the mere transmission of knowledge from expert to novice. This view highlights the importance of the relationship between individual thinking and the social organisation of learning and teaching. It also posits that learners adopt different roles and responsibilities according to the group in which they are participating. Therefore, "learning and development occur as people participate in the sociocultural activities of their community, transforming their understanding, roles, and responsibilities as they participate" (Rogoff, Matusov, & White, 1996, p. 390). For Rogoff and her colleagues, all learning occurs in both cultural and social contexts, with the learner an active member of each context.

In a move away from viewing learning as beginning and ending with the individual (i.e., either transmission of ideas or acquisition of knowledge), the premise of a sociocultural view of learning is that cognitive change is a social and interpersonal process. Arguably, then, this approach explains the learner in a different way from that proposed in other theories of learning. It diverges from a transmission or acquisition model of learning and development, and consequently influences ways in which learners are assessed and evaluated. The sociocultural theory of learning is based on the understanding that people work and learn collaboratively, not individually.

Take a minute to consider either a transmission or an acquisition model of learning and development, where both models have an "active" side and a "passive" side. The world is conceived as active in the former (i.e., transmitting information and knowledge to individuals) and the individual as active in the latter (i.e., actively acquiring knowledge from "outside"). In contrast, the guided participation model, based on the sociocultural theory of learning, proposes that "people change through transforming their *participation* in sociocultural activities—in which both the individual and the rest of the world are active" (Rogoff, 1997, p. 266). Within this perspective, learning is a shared endeavour where learners' ideas are built up in the community of learning, and where learning occurs through participation in varied activities and contexts.

Wood, Bruner, and Ross (1976) use a "scaffolding" metaphor to describe the instructional practices that support learning within the Vygotskian framework—a framework that also draws inspiration from apprenticeships. Scaffolding, with its connotations of mutual support, relates to the concepts of cooperation and collaboration. As we know, through experience "in the real world" and through research, collaboration has to be neither positive nor negative for learning to happen, as even discord can be necessary for learning (Piaget, 1979; Rogoff, 1998). This thinking is evident in the concept of "participation in practice", which has been variously described as guided participation (Rogoff, 1990), legitimate peripheral participation (Lave & Wenger, 1991) and, to a lesser extent, situated learning. All capture the notion that being involved with others in authentic settings for a common purpose supports the learning of all involved, irrespective of the role each person plays.

Approaches to learning

While learning can be defined and conceptualised in various ways according to the underlying theory, the concept of learning and what it means "to learn something" is influenced by the individual's *experience* of learning. In the 1970s, a new research specialisation termed "phenomenography" developed as a means of aiding exploration and understanding of how a student experiences learning from his or her perspective.

Phenomenography

A phenomenographic view of learning is understood as a change of conception resulting from interacting with people or other cultural artefacts (such as computers, books). As a research approach, phenomenography allows us to describe how people experience phenomena in qualitatively different ways. The aim is to describe, analyse and understand experiences through experiential description (Marton, 1981, 1986). The discipline's underlying principle is that the number of qualitatively different ways in which people experience phenomena or aspects of reality (Marton & Booth, 1997) is relatively limited.

Phenomenography originated in Sweden in 1970 when Ference Marton, Lennart Svensson and Roger Säljö began investigating aspects of student learning. The three wanted to focus on the relationship between *what* and *how* students learn rather than on the more favoured position at that time of how much a student had learnt and why. Arguing that the outcome and process of learning are internally related, the group's early studies focused on the relationship between the two (Marton & Säljö, 1976; Marton & Svensson, 1979; Svensson, 1994). As Dall'Alba (1996) later put it, "the learning process and outcome are two aspects of the same whole, rather than separate and distinct phases" (p. 7). This consideration has important implications in educational settings where learning outcomes are formally assessed with no consideration given to the process of learning.

Phenomenographic studies have been useful in identifying the different conceptions that individuals have of learning. The studies include those conducted with young (early childhood) children (Pramling, 1983, 1988), adults (Marton,

Dall'Alba, & Beaty, 1993; Säljö, 1979, 1996), and Years 7 and 8 students (as outlined in this book in Chapters 4 and 6).

In her study of young children, Pramling (1988) reported three conceptions of learning held by the children: learning to do, learning to know the world and learning to understand. In relation to these conceptions, the children identified the *how* of learning as learning as doing, learning by growing older and learning by experience.

Studies by Marton et al. (1993) and Säljö (1979) of adults' conceptions of learning produced six such conceptions. These can be viewed in an hierarchical framework because they move from the least sophisticated and least inclusive (A in the panel below) to the more inclusive and therefore more sophisticated (F in the panel) conceptions of learning. These researchers also linked these "adult" (specifically, adults involved in tertiary education) conceptions of learning to students' approaches to learning. Säljö (1979) identified conceptions A, B or C as those most commonly held by students adopting what he and colleague Marton had earlier described as a *surface* approach to learning (Marton & Säljö, 1976), and conceptions D or E as those held by students adopting a *deep* approach to learning. Other research in this area between 1968 and 1981 identified a third, *strategic* approach to learning (Entwistle, 1987). Each of these three learning approaches link to learning outcomes, but it is the learner's *intention* regarding the learning activity that determines which approach is used.

Phenomenographic conceptions of learning among adult learners

A. Increasing knowledge

B. Memorising and reproducing

C. Applying knowledge

D. Abstracting meaning

E. Seeing something in a different way

F. Changing as a person

These conceptions are drawn from empirical data detailed in studies by Marton et al. (1993) and Säljö (1979). A is the least sophisticated and inclusive conception; F is the most sophisticated and inclusive.

A learner who adopts a *surface approach* to learning is usually intent on completing the assigned task. The task is an end in itself rather than a means to an end. Therefore, the learner usually employs strategies such as rote learning, memorisation and focusing on discrete elements rather than the whole. Surface learning tends to be unreflective, leading to learning outcomes based on reproduction of text (or the content of a lesson) rather than on an interpretation or understanding of the communicative intent of the author. Several other researchers use a similar concept. Gipps (1994), for example, refers to *shallow learning* as "the acquisition of principles from a teacher or other instructor without commitment or deep consideration" (p. 23).

The *deep approach* to learning is associated with the learner's intention to understand the text or activity. The learner interacts with the content of the material and seeks relations between the content and his or her past experiences and prior knowledge. A deep approach to learning depends on prior knowledge of the topic involved (Biggs, 2003).

The *strategic approach* to learning is associated with the learner's intention to maximise grades. The learner is motivated to achieve a desired outcome—higher grades, for instance—rather than to understand the content. The strategic approach is characterised by strategies to promote learning. These include organising time, materials and conditions for studying that are conducive to learning; using strategies such as examining past examination papers for indications as to the likely content and format of future examinations; and generally being alert to cues about marking and assessment schemes.

How students *perceive* a task also influences how they approach learning, how they use their time and how they engage with the tasks presented to them. Students' perceptions of tasks often differ from those of their peers and the teacher, and it is not uncommon for students to complete a task that is different from the one the teacher, or textbook had intended, or even requested. Similarly, research shows that learners presented with the same activity, such as hearing a story, have different ways of recalling and understanding the story. Pramling, Asplund Carlsson, and Klerfelt (1993) describe their study of 96 six-year-old children who were read a story and then interviewed about what they remembered. Some children focused on recall; others on understanding. The authors concluded that learning involves individual interpretations of both the nature of learning per se and the objective of the actual task. Nuthall (1999, 2007) presented a compelling case in support of this conclusion in his study of Years 7 and 8 learners. His findings revealed a remarkable variation in "how" and "what" each child learnt. Even when these learners were "engaged in virtually identical activities, they learned different things in different ways" (Nuthall, 1999, p. 305).

This often marked difference between teachers' and school students' perceptions of work suggests the need for a high level of negotiation in teacher–student interactions. Ramsden (1988) found that tertiary students also tend to "react to educational situations differently from the ways teachers or experimenters predict. This is because they react to the requirements *they* perceive, not always the ones we define" (p. 24).

Learning and context

The setting or context for learning has a marked impact on how students learn and their performance on an activity (McNamee & Sivright, 2002; Petrone, 2010). Perceptions of children's learning ability can differ according to whether the children are assessed in *authentic* contexts or "school-based" settings. Drawing on an earlier study of Brazilian street-vendor children, Ceci and Roazzi (1994) showed that the performance of the children on a number of Piagetian tasks differed according to context. The authors examined two contexts: (1) the street as an authentic context for the children while selling their wares; and (2) a formalised testing situation involving Piagetian tasks that corresponded to those asked within the vendor context. The children were more successful when working within the authentic context than the formalised, superficial setting, confirming earlier research findings (e.g., Donaldson, 1978; Pramling, 1990) which showed that the Piagetian stages (sensorimotor, pre-operational, concrete operational, formal operational) depend on both content and context.

Lave, Murtaugh, and de la Rocha (1984) illustrate this point further. During their study of adult shoppers, they observed "virtually error free arithmetic performance" by people when acting as shoppers but frequent errors in parallel problems in the formal testing situation (p. 83). Shoppers achieved a 98 percent correction rate for solving arithmetic problems within the supermarket setting but a 59 percent success rate with similar problems in an arithmetic test. Boaler (1993) likewise argued that the context in which mathematics takes place is a factor in determining how students approach the task and therefore the learning outcome generated from their chosen approach.

There is other evidence that learning is closely linked to the circumstances of its acquisition (Billett, 1996; Säljö & Wyndhamn, 1993). Säljö and Wyndhamn (1993), for example, examined the influence of context on solving the same problem—working out postal rates for sending a letter—in two different classes. The students were presented with both the problem and the postal-rate table. Some students were given the task within the context of a mathematics class; the other students within the context of a social studies class. The authors found that the students' perception of the task influenced the way they approached it. Within the mathematics context, 57.4 percent of the students interpreted the problem as a mathematical task and so engaged in some kind of calculation. However, only 29.3 percent of the students in the social studies context used mathematical operations to arrive at an answer.

Matusov, Bell, and Rogoff (2002) studied collaborative problem solving with children (9- to 11-year-olds) in out-of-school contexts. The students were from two different schools. The first encouraged collaboration and made it part of the school culture. The second held to a traditional individual learner model with minimal emphasis on collaboration. The researchers paired the children, with each pair comprising students from the same school. They asked one child from each pair to teach the other child a specified task. Children from the collaborative school used strategies such as collaboration, consensus decision making and building on one another's ideas to achieve their goals. The children from the traditional school did not appear to use these strategies, but instead employed more didactic approaches with their peers. This study suggests that the school environment and structures influence how children work with each other in out-of-school settings.

School learning differs from the type of learning that occurs through everyday activities (Harlen, 2006; Lave, 1988). Recognising different learning contexts is important in supporting learner motivations (Harlen, 2006). For example, a study by Skilton-Sylvester (2002) showed a marked difference in the performance of a young Cambodian child in Philadelphia with regard to her school writing and her out-of-school writing. Her writing in the former situation was assessed for accuracy. In the latter, where she performed better, a component of the writing linked to a subsequent oral performance. As a result, for this child, "the resources she brought to school were often invisible or devalued" (p. 65).

In short, research over a number of years shows the way we learn in everyday settings is substantially removed from the type of learning encouraged in school settings (see also Gardner, 1991; Harlen, 2006; Lave, 1988; Rogoff & Lave, 1984).

School learning

Learning within school systems and in out-of-school settings is structured differently, a situation that affects the learner's view of the *why* and *how* of learning (Marton & Booth, 1996, 1997). Säljö and Wyndhamn (1993) argue that schools "provide external conditions or learning activities that differ from those that exist when these activities are embedded in the routines of activities in other social settings" (p. 328). Learning at school involves cultural practices that are, often through necessity, institutionalised. The associated traditions within many school settings have not changed for years, and still remain "somewhat predictable, normative, and structural" (Matusov et al., 2002, p. 131).

Learning, and engaging students with learning, is not problematic if there is a match between learner motivation and choice for action; however, the institutional processes required to operate schools *are* problematic, in part because they are set up to formalise the process of learning and cultural reproduction (Foucault, 1977). As Matusov et al. (2002) identify, schools provide contexts where structure, rules and systematised activity constitute learning, and where rules are seen as "cultural tools". A study (Méard, Bertone, & Flavier, 2008) that looked at how six- to eight-year-olds negotiated and internalised rules showed how quickly young children internalise "rules" at school (e.g., getting to class on time, not speaking unless being called to, lining up). There are rules for learning to read, learning to write, how to hold a pencil, and there are rules governing academic subjects. Some rules are explicit and others are negotiated daily by teacher and learner (Méard et al., 2008). Within any secondary school timetable, rules are also evident through structured, regulated time and content that leads the pattern of learning opportunities. However, the activities of teaching and learning are never predictable because the process of teaching is itself under constant transformation:

> The context of teaching is always vague, inexact, and changing. The classroom is not the same in the fall as it is in the spring, or in the morning as it is in the afternoon. Students' and teachers' moods change throughout the day. Students become and cease being discipline problems, but exactly when it is sometimes difficult to say. The effect of our teaching cannot be determined. We may have taught well, but the results will not reveal themselves until next year in Mr. Robb's class. Above all, students grow. If they did not, then there would be no reason to teach. (Garrison, 1997, p. 5)

Rules are not, of course, confined to school-based settings. Young people quickly establish what the "rules" are in any given context. For example, Petrone (2010) in his study of out-of-school learning in a skateboard park uses the words of a young skateboarder to explain that "there is no easy way to learn that [the unwritten rules of how to use the park]. You have to get hit a couple of times" (p. 119). The way young people engage in a learning activity is influenced by the messages portrayed about learning through the varied cultures and systems within which they learn. Given that a school activity exists in a culture of its own (Lave, 1988), and given that there are many aspects of that culture (Alton-Lee & Nuthall, 1992), teachers, when facilitating student learning, must recognise such cultures. One aspect of the school culture relevant to learning and identity is that of peers.

The role of peers in the learning process

Within a school setting, students learn, play and work alongside their peers, so creating a unique student culture. The positive effect of peers on the learning process is enhanced when these peers are also friends (Berndt & Keefe, 1992; Zajac & Hartup, 1997). Vygotsky's notion of "another" in the mediation of learning is important, but so too is the *quality* of the relationship between the child and peers. Friends working together benefit one another. Children know their friends, and are therefore likely to accept their suggestions, explanations and comments. Friends generally have a strong commitment to one another that facilitates learning. Because friends tend to feel more secure with one another, the affective climate is more favourable for exploring tasks and solving problems. Children manage conflicts more effectively with their friends.

Research shows that peers can influence the way students *approach* a learning task (Filer, 1997; Nuthall, 1999, 2007). For example, Filer (1997) reported that students presenting their "news" in class experienced a tension between either giving "deviant comedy" to please their peers or providing a news story that would please their teacher. Students develop their own subculture within the classroom setting. Often distinct from any formalised school culture, this serves to establish identity and status between peers (Woods, 1990), and provides a means of rejecting adult culture (Metcalf & Hunt, 1974). This is achieved in various ways, including the use of nicknames, humour and jokes. As Woods (1990) notes:

> To be member of a group, a child must have a nickname, usually 'short and snappy' and 'playfully affectionate', and their use helps to cement the bonds of the group. Those with no nicknames are social outcasts. Those with nasty nicknames, like some of the teachers, are members of opposing groups. (p. 197)

Peers within a school-based setting can thus negatively or positively affect both learning and student identity (Martino & Pallotta-Chiarolli, 2007).

Out-of-school learning

Increasingly, research is portraying the considerable achievement of young learners in out-of-school settings, and of the same learners not achieving within school settings (e.g., Guerra & Farr, 2002; Hull & Schultz, 2002; McNamee & Sivright, 2002). In early studies, a distinction was made between school and out-of-school learning with regard to the focus of the learning: "schooling focuses on the individual's performance, whereas out-of-school mental work is often socially shared" (Resnick, 1987, p. 84). The more recent research focused on knowledge created and valued within different contexts (e.g., Hull & Schultz, 2002) shows that home and community contexts, which often value ways of knowing different from those promoted at school, frequently legitimate out-of-school learning. Hull and Shultz (2002) argue that knowledge gained, and valued, out of school needs to be transformed profitably into a school context, for both learner and teacher. Resnick (1987) reminds us that an effective learner in a school context will not necessarily be equipped with essential learning skills in out-of-school contexts: "As long as school focuses mainly on individual forms of competence, on tool-free performance, and on decontextualised skills, educating people to be good learners in school settings alone may not be sufficient to help them become strong out-of-school learners" (p. 86).

For teachers, finding ways of recognising out-of-school knowledge is a challenge, not only because they are pressured to *measure* certain forms of learning, despite curriculum reforms aiming to create "confident, connected, actively involved, and lifelong learners" (Ministry of Education, 2007, p. 8), but also because some students' out-of-school experiences are not readily understood in a school context (Johnston & Nicholls, 1995; Jones, 1991; Skilton-Sylvester, 2002; Thiessen & Cook-Sather, 2007).

In a New Zealand study of female secondary school students, Jones (1991) observed that how girls talked about school and their role within school differed markedly from how they talked about their lives and roles outside school. The girls viewed out-of-school experiences as irrelevant to school, and saw the two contexts as quite separate. Johnston and Nicholls (1995) drew on this work when investigating their belief that students have many voices, some of which are silenced in a school setting. Research on how student voice can influence, challenge and contribute to policy and practice continues to highlight the disparity between what students *think* about schooling and how "the system" perceives them; and how this disparity can alienate some students from learning (Mitra, 2004; Rudduck, 2007).

The way parents and caregivers teach their children also contributes to out-of-school learning. That teaching, say of a subject such as science, is in turn, influenced by the home culture and the parents' conceptualisations of science and education (Solomon, 1994). Chavajay and Rogoff's (1999) study set in a Guatemalan Mayan community and a European community in the United States explored how mothers and their toddlers (14 to 20 months of age) attended to a variety of tasks and activities around them. The authors distinguished between simultaneous attention and alternating attention. Simultaneous attention involved the child or adult responding to several different things at once, whereas alternating attention involved changing the attention or becoming distracted and attending to only one thing at a time. The Mayan parents and their toddlers were more likely to attend simultaneously to competing events, whereas the European families tended to alternate attention between competing events; thus, differences in how people respond to a number of tasks are likely to be related to differences in the community in which they are raised (see also Rogoff, Paradise, Mejía Arauz, Correa-Chávez, & Angelillo, 2003). Learning is undoubtedly a phenomenon embedded in the cultural, historical and social world of the learner and the community.

Summary

The way we learn has a powerful impact on approaches to learning and the outcomes of learning. Learning is a cognitive, social and cultural process that occurs within a community of practice. While formalised learning occurs predominantly in a school setting, learning also occurs in diverse, everyday settings. The setting influences learners' responses to the learning activity, and it emphasises the role of students and how they see themselves in the learning process. Teachers able to recognise how their students learn and understand their learning will help those students become "better learners". As Pramling (1996) says, "If we want to know what characterises children's learning, we must know how they see it from their own perspective. And if our knowledge about children's learning should make children better 'learners', we must develop their understanding of their own learning" (p. 565). However, to do this as educators we must first understand how students conceptualise and experience learning.

In out-of-school contexts, learning occurs in authentic and natural settings where students' performance of tasks is often better than when they undertake similar tasks in a school setting. Students approach learning in school with this vast background of experience, yet this learning is not readily acknowledged in a school setting. To develop effective teaching and assessment systems in schools, we need to explore how students learn and self-assess, and how the settings in which assessment and learning occur contribute to the way students approach such tasks. As a starting point, the following chapter provides an overview of students' conceptions of learning.

CHAPTER 4

Students and their learning

> The standard view of the classroom is that the teacher provides students with a set of activities. Some students do the activities well and learn more ... The assumption seems to be that all students experience essentially the same activities, and perform them according to their motivation or ability ... It is also assumed that learning is the more or less automatic result of engaging in classroom activities. If students do what the teacher expects of them, follow the instructions carefully, complete all aspects of the tasks, then the students will learn what the teacher expects ... *our research shows that almost none of this is true.* (Nuthall, 2007, p. 103, emphasis added)

In this quotation, what does Nuthall mean by "true"? Apparently, the intricate combinations of students' motivation, background, skill, peer relationships, status, task engagement, teachers and activities mean no two children learn alike, and no individual student learns in the same way across activities, even in the same classroom. When we, as teachers and researchers, talk about children's learning, we are often not talking about the same thing. Experienced and effective teachers know intuitively "when it works". Good teachers support student learning without necessarily being conscious of doing one particular thing. While we can define and distil ideas about what makes teaching effective, doing so is not the same as knowing how best to support student learning. This chapter focuses on one key question: What are Year 7 students' conceptions of learning?

The best part about exploring the what and the how of learning with young people is that they truly do not have the answers. Nor, for that matter, do we as teachers or researchers. Between us, we come to understand some things. An insight into the variation in students' conceptions of learning gives us further insight into learning itself.

Studying students' conceptions of learning

The 26 students (15 males and 11 females) who feature in this chapter were from three Year 7 classes in one intermediate school. Their ages ranged from 10.3 years to 12.3 years. Over three months, I interviewed each student. Each interview took from 35 to 60 minutes to complete, depending on how fast the student spoke and the amount of information each student wanted to share.

In this chapter, I include extracts from the student interviews as examples of the categories of description that I developed from my analysis of the transcripts. As I noted earlier in this book, the categories move from the least sophisticated and least inclusive views to the most sophisticated and most inclusive views, resulting in hierarchical models of conceptions of learning. I explain these in detail to show how students think about learning in very different ways, and how their school-based notions of learning are often less sophisticated than their out-of-school conceptions. The examples reinforce the view that there is no single, right way in which students think about learning: each way creates a view of learning that we, as teachers and researchers, need to understand. Through these young people's varied and graphic portrayals of learning, we can start to see learning in another way—their way.

Students' conceptions of learning

The categories of description of learning summarised in the following panel range from acquiring knowledge (A) to seeing something in a different way (E). A common question representing the students' views is included with each

Students' conceptions of learning	
A. Acquiring knowledge	Learning is about gathering facts from the teacher or other sources (books, computers) to "fill up the brain". The learner relies on the teacher to present learning material. This category is characterised by the question: *What do I need to know?*
B. Memorising and reproducing	Learning is seen as a collation of facts to be recalled at a later date. The student uses repetitive techniques to practise skills acquired. Learners believe there is only one solution to a problem. They see regurgitation of facts as an indicator of learning, and that this process is achieved through constant practice (rote learning). This category is characterised by the question: *What do I need to remember?*
C. Using your knowledge	Learning is viewed as the ability to apply knowledge with increasing degrees of speed and accuracy. The learner sees ability to complete work as an aspect of learning, and considers improvement in learning as ability to complete work faster and more accurately. This category is characterised by the question: *How do I do this?*
D. Understanding	Learning is viewed as understanding the problem. Students use prior learning to solve problems and see learning connections, rather than as activities in isolation. Students know what they want to achieve, and they see repetition of similar work as unnecessary and boring. They use practice as an intentional strategy to develop their understanding and skills. These students view learning as involving teaching others, and drawing on peers to facilitate understanding. This category is characterised by the question: *How do I use this information?*
E. Different ways of knowing	Learning is viewed as exciting. Students recognise different ways of knowing about things, and look for different perspectives when solving a problem. This category is characterised by the question: *How can I solve this problem?*

conception. For example, students with the least sophisticated conception of learning (A) asked the hypothetical question, "What do I need to know?" The question for the most sophisticated category of learning (E) was "How can I solve this problem?"

In general, the students in this study referred to learning in school settings. I used two questions to elicit discussion on other settings:
- Does learning happen in places other than school?
- Does learning happen anywhere else?

In answer, the students referred to three forms of out-of-school settings. One involved structured learning of a school-related nature but not occurring in the school grounds, such as school camps. The most prominent setting identified involved structured learning that was not school-related, such as judo, dancing, karate and art classes. The other out-of-school settings that the students referred to tended to involve situations that were unstructured and unplanned but where learning nonetheless occurred. These were activities at home; for example, fence making on the farm, caring for animals, looking after siblings and learning to use equipment such as the television's remote control.

Students who stated they were actively involved in out-of-school learning experiences and who gave examples of learning activities in such settings tended to hold more sophisticated conceptions of learning when discussing learning in these contexts. However, their views of learning within a school setting often represented a less sophisticated conception, a finding that suggests the context of school-based learning encourages or facilitates particular views on learning. Consequently, the students saw the need to reproduce information in tests as an important aspect of school-related learning, and they were keen to memorise information so they could demonstrate their learning. In contrast, the students characterised the out-of-school learning experiences they described as ones involving choice, voluntary participation and active participation. In these contexts, students seemed less concerned about regurgitating information and more concerned about performing appropriately. To do this, they needed to understand what they were attempting, and it is perhaps this aspect of the activity that contributed to their more sophisticated conceptions of learning.

These conceptions were represented by students who viewed understanding as an important attribute of learning (Category D) and who used this understanding to identify different ways of knowing, to see things in different ways and/or to identify multiple perspectives when solving problems (E). One of the main differences between these two conceptions of learning (D and E) and the less sophisticated conceptions (A, B, C) was the way students identified with and used prior knowledge. Students who discussed learning as understanding or as identifying multiple perspectives also talked about using their knowledge to solve problems or to understand the material. In contrast, students who saw learning as acquiring knowledge (A), reproducing material (B) and/or applying the knowledge (C) tended to talk as if all knowledge was new to them; they did not refer to incorporating existing knowledge or experience.

Acquiring knowledge (A): What do I need to know?

The students in this, the least sophisticated category, viewed learning as the way to gain knowledge. "Gaining knowledge" was a component inherent in all subsequent categories, and acted as a prerequisite for the more inclusive conceptions.

With this category students believed they started school with a near empty brain that required filling. As one said, "You don't know anything when you're born." Some also said that the brain, and therefore knowledge, grows with age. Within this category, students described learning as a process of "getting to know" some school-related content—content that they believed increased with age—while also acknowledging the role of learning in acquiring this knowledge.

The student in the following extract explains that her brain was empty when she was born, and that learning is the process required to fill it up. However, she differentiates between two sections of her brain, nominating one side for learning and the other for movement:

> S: *I think it's, well, like, because when we're born we have a brain and all it does is make our body move, and it's kind of empty, and we need something to fill it up, so they teach us skills of learning, and then we can go out and get a job and we know how to do things like that.*
> R: *Can you tell me more about the brain that's empty?*
> S: *There's two halves. One half is used for moving your body, and then the other half is for your learning; it's kind of empty until you fill it up.*

When I asked how "full" her brain presently was, she replied:

Probably about half full, no, it's probably about, oh a ... an eighth full probably, because I've already just started kind of learning. Through high school it might be just about a quarter or half full, and then you get your job, and it's half full, and you keep learning, and it gets to full almost, and then it starts going down again when you get old. It probably still holds all that information, but you just don't use it as much because you don't have a job anymore, you retire.

I found that when students think about learning mainly as a process of gathering outside knowledge to "fill the brain" or "store in the brain", they approach learning in specific ways. They also see themselves in a particular way that involves minimising their identity as a learner. For example, they say they "don't know" a lot, and rather than focusing on what they can do and how they can build on their current understanding, they look at what is "out there" and mainly see knowledge that is not accessible to them. This conception puts them, as learners, in a relatively powerless state.

Students who held conceptions within this category also tended to believe teachers' knowledge is imparted to them to the extent that they (the students) no longer have to think about it. For example:

Well, every day, they [the teachers] keep putting something in your mind, and then they keep enforcing it, and then they start with something new at the end. So, after about a week, you don't have to think about it.

For these students, the teacher's role is to provide students with the knowledge, facts and information they are required to learn. Students also believed it was this knowledge that would be evaluated and assessed at a later stage. They not only saw teachers as a major source of information, but also saw external forms of knowledge as coming from other sources, including books, computers and the library. The significance of this conception of learning is that students see themselves and the information they are to acquire as separate entities that are joined by learning instigated by the teacher.

Students expressed these views of learning only when talking about learning in school. When referring to experiences outside school, not one student expressed a Category A conception of learning.

Memorising and reproducing (B): What do I need to remember?

The students in this category (B) talked about remembering and reproducing knowledge, information and/or ideas. However, some saw this process as a means to an end and tried to understand how the process worked, while others saw it in terms of rote learning. This latter group had no understanding of how and why they memorised information. The students featuring in this category were those who *mainly* held this conception, and who tended not to hold more sophisticated conceptions. They were the students who viewed learning as a process directed at reproducing information.

This category is more sophisticated than Category A because the students in it have moved from the notion of simply acquiring knowledge in order to fill one's mind to the notion of developing a strategy to retain the knowledge:

- *You've got to remember how to do things, and the right way.*
- *You know the answer ... you actually know it because it's in your brain so you don't forget it.*
- *With school work, your brain thinks, 'Right, we'll call up the memory,' and they write it down on the paper inside your head.*

Some of the students within this category believed the knowledge was already within them, and that it was through reproducing it that they came to learn. As one student said, her knowledge "just stays there and waits until you need it ... [before I] let it out". In similar vein, the students tended to speak of remembering as a strategy to store information in the brain, which, according to one student, "gets bigger and bigger". This student said that when he wanted to remember information, he needed to retrieve it from a specific place in his brain:

> R: Can you tell me what remembering is, then?
> S: Well, it's just you store it in the back of your brain.
> R: Oh, okay. How much storage space do you have?
> S: As much as I like.
> R: How does that work?
> S: Um, it just gets bigger and bigger every time.
> R: So your brain's getting bigger and bigger?
> S: Yeah, as well as me.

R: *Oh, I see, it grows with you?*

S: *Yeah. It's just like my sister's best friend. Jenson. He is, like, seven foot, and he's still growing. He'll be able to go Michael Jordan slam dunk.*

R: *So you keep remembering things by storing it in the back of your brain?*

S: *Yeah. Like when I just want the information, I just think of it, and it comes out into the front of my brain.*

R: *Oh, I see. So when you use it, it goes to the front of your brain?*

S: *Yeah. When I don't use it, it goes to the back.*

R: *Well, where does learning fit into that?*

S: *It fits on the right-hand side.*

Another student emphasised the importance of remembering in learning:

You need to remember, like, you need to remember what eight times nine is and all that, otherwise you will never succeed. Sometimes at night when I can't get a maths problem, I just keep on saying it in my head. I write down on a piece of paper at night, and I read it, and I say it out loud, then I cover it over and say it in my head, then I say it out loud and see if I get the answer right.

For these students, the purpose of remembering was to recall information for a test or assessment. They identified memorisation as an important strategy relative to test taking, and generally did not associate remembering with increased understanding. As the student in the following example explained, the motivation to remember what had been learnt arose because the knowledge was to be evaluated by the teacher. Learning, for this student, was about reproducing information:

S: *When something, like, sometimes when we're doing a test, I just remember—like for the Sioux, I had to remember that they lived on the plains and they used to be farmers, so I just kept saying it in my mind.*

R: *That they lived where?*

S: *That they lived on the plains in America, and they used to be farmers that lived on the hills.*

R: *And why did you have to know that?*

S: *Because the teacher was going to ask us questions the next day.*

This student had earlier described learning as the process of "shoving it in your brain" so that when teachers ask questions, students know the answer:

S: *Yeah, because, you can, like, the teacher will ask you a question, and you can remember it, so you've shoved it in your brain, you've learnt it—you understand it.*
R: *Oh, you understand it?*
S: *Yeah. You know what's going on, sort of thing, like you've learnt it—it's stuck in your brain.*

Within this category, the process of memorising appeared to hold two main functions for the students. One was to learn more of or about a specific skill or concept, and the other was to remember or retain the information. Students referred to both as indicators of learning. When I asked a student who believed learning was filling up the brain, she explained how this happened:

R: *How do you fill it [your brain] up?*
S: *By listening to the teacher and practising what you've learnt, like in maths, if you practise what you've learnt that day you might, you fill it up more and if you practise your times tables and get them all down.*

However, as one student noted, memorising does not always work. She explained that she practised something until it was "fixed" in her mind. She used as an example her learning of superlatives in English, but when she attempted to explain them, found she was unable to do so. This example illustrates how students who view learning within this conception do not realise the importance of understanding or applying the information if they are to retain it; instead, they believe retention of knowledge is based on repetition and memorisation.

In this category, students used memorising and repetition to increase their ability to recall information. Their belief was that "knowing it off by heart" in a variety of curriculum areas, such as science, spelling, mathematics and physical education, requires practice and repetition:

You're supposed to practise and practise and practise until you really remember it. Like, if you learn your times tables, you can't just learn it once and forget about it or else you'll never have them in your head. Like, you have to kind of practise and practise and practise, and then you'll know it off by heart.

Listening was viewed as a significant part of learning and, along with practice, was mentioned by students as a useful strategy to "get better" at a learning task. One student, for example, used the metaphor of a tape recorder to describe the function of learning, which, he explained, is an ongoing process of taking in information. The students who identified learning mainly as increasing one's knowledge typically considered "listening and taking in the information" to be important:

> S: Well, you wouldn't really know that you're learning, you're just, like, doing it in your mind. Your mind's like a tape recorder, like, that we're on now, and it just takes in the information, and you don't even really know you've got it. That's how I find it.
> R: That's interesting. So, like, your tape recorder's on, and so things are going in all the time are they?
> S: Yeah.
> R: How do you know if you're recording something then?
> S: You're mostly recording something all the time because, like, I'll remember talking to you now, so I've basically recorded it because I've remembered I've been talking to you.
> R: And where does it all go?
> S: Into your mind. Well, when you teach, you're doing, you're, like, making someone learn when you teach. When you're learning, you're, like, you're not the person teaching them, you're the person, like, listening and taking in the information, so you're the tape recorder.

When viewing learning as memorisation, students also talked about speed and accuracy of recall as an index of "getting better"—at learning. This view was particularly evident when students mentioned spelling and mathematics. In the following example, the student explains his use of races in mathematics (a strategy established by the teacher) to determine his learning progress:

> S: Maths, I've gotten better at my times tables.
> R: And how did you get better at your times tables?
> S: We do a race with, um, times, and we put ten numbers along the top and ten down the side, and we have to fill in all the gaps in five minutes ... and when you've finished, you say, 'Stop,' and the teacher gives you your time.
> R: So what are you trying to do?
> S: Trying to improve your times tables and learn them so you can, um, say them faster, know them off by heart.
> R: What's the difference between knowing something off by heart, like your times tables, and learning your times table?

> S: *Knowing them off by heart you can, someone can just ask you a question and you can just say it like that, and if you don't know it off by heart, you take a while to give them an answer. If you get a time, and then the next day you get a faster time, that means you're learning them.*

One of the strategies the students reported using to retain information was mnemonics. But again, this example highlighted the tendency for these students to conflate remembering and recalling with learning; they did not see learning as understanding. In the following extract, the student recognises the importance of remembering phrases and words. He had earlier explained to me that a series of lessons on health had introduced him to unfamiliar words. With his mother's help, he adopted a strategy of using a word he knew to remember one he did not. However, his idea of memorising helped him only to remember the word; the idea of understanding the subject matter held little priority or relevance for him. Nor did he see this as the focus of learning. For him, the focus was remembering the word:

> *Well, when they're telling you something, you can write down notes and then go home and memorise it, or you can just say the word over and over again in your mind until you get that word, and you already know what it is. When he says something about puberty I, um, memorise words so I know what I'm talking about and, then, and then I know exactly what it does because of what the word is and what you're associating with. And then that's how you learn things, and then they say, 'Oh no, don't you mean it's a different name?' or something, like fallopian tube, and I couldn't get that right. What I remember words by is from other words. Like, what about a vulva? I remember it by revolver for a gun, because a revolver is an easier word to remember for me.*

Using your knowledge (C): How do I do this?

When learners move beyond wanting to know and remember, they begin to use their knowledge and to view and enjoy learning in a broader way. This third category, C, is more sophisticated than Categories A and B because the learners have moved from acquiring knowledge and developing a strategy to retain that knowledge to applying the knowledge to a particular task. While components of

Categories A and B are precursors to Category C, the distinguishing feature of this category is the learners' understanding that they are applying their skills and knowledge to new problems. Thus, for these learners, being able to complete a task equates with learning.

The need for tests and assessment information, evident in Categories A and B, is also part of this conception of learning, but is not so strong in focus. While class tests helped the students who held this conception "identify" or "confirm" their own learning, they generally used this information in an intentional way. In the following example, the student differentiates between completing a test and using the information practically. It is the *use* of the information that identifies his view of learning as a Category C conception, because, as he notes, he wanted to see if what he had learnt was "real":

> *You've got to go through tests and see whatever you've learnt, if it's real, [but] you've got to be sure that you can do it as well.*

Another student explained that she knew when she had misspelt a word and did not need a test to confirm her judgement. While her approach represents self-assessment, it also demonstrates her link with Category C learning:

> *If you're spelling something, you know the word just looks wrong. Even if you've just got one letter in the wrong place, you know it just doesn't look right.*

In Category C, the purpose of learning shifts from recalling knowledge for tests or to complete a task to that of applying knowledge in a more conceptual manner. Essentially, learners in this category view the *process* of learning differently. They no longer focus on memorising or remembering information but on using that information intentionally, for some purpose. As the student below explains, she learnt to spell a word by *using* it rather than memorising it, unlike students who conceptualise learning in Category B, who associate spelling with memorising:

> *Like, for spelling, then you usually know if you've learnt the word, but quite often, you know, I forget the spelling word after about a month. But ... say I'm doing a project on something, and I use that word often, then I'm learning by that way, and then I've usually learnt it by writing a whole page, using the word in every few sentences. And I've learnt it then.*

When students begin to understand that their prior knowledge assists further learning, they become more engaged as learners. They feel more in control of the learning process and, unlike students who conceptualise learning in Categories A and B, do not see learning as accumulating information from "out there":

Well, when you memorise things, you actually learn, you still learn because you already know that, and you develop knowledge for yourself, and that is what's going to help you more—knowledge, getting information and starting to use it. And, because, if you get that knowledge, you can use it in other situations.

The conception that learning is the application of knowledge is further demonstrated in the following example. This student had learnt to use a protractor in mathematics:

S: When we were told how to use a protractor, they'd [the teacher] just sort of show us where we'd put it, and it would come up with all the lines coming off the protractor, and it would show you how many degrees in an angle.
R: So when the teacher showed you, is that when you'd learnt it?
S: Yeah, and then we'd get a worksheet and we'd have to try it out ourselves.
R: Okay and when you go and try it out yourself, did you know that you'd learnt it then?
S: I was just sort of making sure that I knew how to do it in case someone put it in front of me and I had to do it straight away or something.
R: So how do you make sure that you can do it?
S: You just answer the questions and you just, at the end they are marking and if you get them all right you think, yeah I'm on my way.

This student's "I'm on my way" phrase not only indicated she was moving towards a more advanced understanding of learning but it was also consistent with terminology used by other students who held this conception. They were aware of being able to do something, such as use a protractor, and although they did not necessarily understand the underlying principle of what they were doing or why they were doing it, they were aware they had more to learn. In contrast, students holding primarily Category B views and able to use protractors would consider they had learnt all about this tool and would not be aware that their understanding of its application was limited.

There was evidence from the transcripts that students who identified with a Category C conception of learning held this conception in places other than school. When talking about learning in these settings, their descriptions highlighted the ability to perform a task as an indicator of learning; they saw this ability as "learning". They also distinguished compulsory learning at school from voluntary participation in out-of-school or home learning situations. As the boy below said, a student can say, "I don't want to do this any more" when at home, but not at school:

> S: *At school some of the time, it's boring and some of the time it's fun, and whenever you're at home, it's always fun because you like doing it, because you can just give up on it whenever you like—so if it's boring, you just say, 'I don't want to do this any more,' and you just give up on it and do something else.*
> R: *But you can't do that at school?*
> S: *No, you have to do it, otherwise you'd get a detention or something like that.*

Similarly, one student stated with regard to out-of-school learning activities:

> *You've got to look forward to it, and you're not doing it because someone wants you to do it. You want to do it because you want to.*

Another student alluded to voluntary participation in other settings when explaining why he did not enjoy school:

> *I don't really like school. It takes six hours of your day up, and then you've got homework, that's wasting all your time, your freedom.*

Learning in out-of-school settings appeared to involve the students in more practical learning experiences. One student said that in contrast to acquiring a product while shopping in her community, she acquired nothing other than knowledge when studying mathematics at school:

> *Like, if you learn about money and stuff, and you've got enough money to learn how much it costs to buy it, well, then it's good because then you get something. Because, like, in maths, you don't get actually something, you just get the knowledge—that's real boring.*

Here, she distinguished between *doing* something, which is consistent with a Category C conception of learning, and *acquiring* something (Category A). She placed more value on the purchasing power of money than on her knowledge in mathematics at school, but ironically did not see the connection between the two.

Another student, when describing learning how to make a fence on her father's farm, told me of her thumb-test: she measured her learning in terms of her ability to hammer in staples without hitting her thumb. The specific skill of hammering—of hitting the staple, not her thumb, by keeping her wrist still—was her indicator for learning. But note in the next extract that she does not indicate an understanding of the finer details associated with making a fence, as might be seen in a more sophisticated conception of learning:

> R: What about at home, when you said you're learning at home, what sort of things are you learning?
> S: Well, dad lives out on the farm, so you're learning how to get on with the sheep and build fences and stuff like that.
> R: Really, have you learnt to build a fence?
> S: Yeah, kind of.
> R: How did you learn that?
> S: Because dad's a builder, and so he just builds fences around the place, and I help him.
> R: What sorts of things have you learnt out of that?
> S: Just skills, how to, and timing and that, and keeping your wrist still, and when you're hammering, you can't move your wrist.
> R: So there's quite a skill to hammering?
> S: Yeah.
> R: When you learnt that, how did you know when you've learnt it?
> S: I didn't hit my thumb.
> R: How can you see progress? How do you figure out progress?
> S: Well, when we're making the fences, like, at the start I kept hitting my thumb and stuff but at the end I could do it without hitting my hands.

In general, students who discussed learning in out-of-school settings saw beyond the acquisition of factual information. That they did so was partly because of how they undertook their leisure activities and out-of-school learning, which were usually practical in nature and, in the students' words, fun.

Understanding (D): How do I use this information?

Learners who aim for understanding when they learn, and who want to feel confident when applying this understanding to new problems, show a more sophisticated conception of learning. No longer are they merely looking to memorise (Category B) or apply the knowledge (Category C). Instead, they are seeking meaning in information and knowledge. Learning has gone beyond the stage of acquisition or recall, and also beyond the stage of applying the knowledge. In Category D, learners want to engage actively to understand new information, and to actively link that information to what they already know and understand. They want to be able to *use* it. A student wanting to know how to hammer in a nail without hitting her thumb (Category C) has a different conception of learning from a student who wants to know what other purposes hammering can be used for (Category D), purposes that she may not even be aware of, such as tapping framing timbers into position or loosening rusted joints.

When learners reach the point of conceptualising learning as understanding, they understand their current knowledge, and the relevance of that knowledge to the task. This is a more sophisticated conception than those in Categories A to C because these learners are beginning to understand they already have a great deal of knowledge and that learning is about developing that knowledge so they can put it to use. Within this conception, learners have an inherent interest in the task they are performing, and they relate it to their own understanding of the activity.

In the following extract, a student discusses the importance of using interesting words in his poetry writing. He says that he uses the dictionary to find their meanings so he can use them in a particular way in his writing. Earlier in the interview, he had explained that books helped him to learn and introduced him to interesting words. He then found out what these words meant and used them in his poetry:

> R: *What would be an example of one of those interesting words?*
> S: *Like extraordinary, slithery and all those interesting and long words.*
> R: *So when you've learnt something like extraordinary or slithery, what do you do with those words?*

S: *I go and check in the dictionary to see what they mean, and then I remember them if they're, like, good words, like good to use. So, when I write a poem or something, then I can use them.*

Within a school setting, students become accustomed to completing many tasks with similar functions. This is particularly so in mathematics and spelling, where work is typically repetitive and focuses on practising certain skills or rules. When students are asked to complete unnecessary numbers of examples in mathematics or written language, they often report learning as boring. The student quoted below, knowing he does not need to complete numerous examples to develop his understanding of a task, describes it as *boring*:

R: *So what do you mean by boring?*
S: *Like, when you just have to do reading and just write out answers for it, when you know that they're all going to be right exactly, and you know everything all right, and you, like, just revision, but it's too much revision when you know what you're doing all the time. It's too much to do and it's too easy.*
R: *Ah, so boring learning is when it's too easy?*
S: *Yeah, really too easy. Really, really, really easy.*

The students who saw learning as understanding, perhaps of a problem or a culture, also discussed the need to learn concepts that held special interest for them, as the next extract illustrates. In response to a question, the student replied that he wanted to learn more about the ancient Egyptians. Note that his interest was not on factual information, but on understanding what life was like during this time:

S: *Mmm, how the ancient Egyptians lived, but without the years and dates and stuff like that—just how they lived. Yes.*
R: *Why does that interest you?*
S: *I just find it amazing how they made a civilization so early and then later after that, like Middle Ages, it was just destroyed. I mean, because it was harder in ancient Egypt than, say, Middle Ages somewhere in Europe.*

The students who held a conception of learning in Category D also identified learning activities in out-of-school settings as "learning as understanding". The need to memorise at a superficial level and to recall knowledge at speed are not features of this conception of learning. More typical is the ability to perform while understanding the intention behind the task. When talking about out-of-school learning experiences, these students identified with this conception because the practical activities associated with these contexts encouraged them to apply their skills and knowledge.

This association with practice to increase performance and ability resembles the strategy students use to regurgitate information in academic settings (Category B), but it is a more sophisticated view of learning because students use practice as an intentional strategy to facilitate performance or understanding. Earlier in this book, I mentioned the skill of counting to 10 in Japanese. In the following extract, a student describes doing just this for his judo class. It was evident during the interview that he needed to understand the words to use them correctly, and therefore needed to learn them through repetition, but *with meaning*. He also monitored his own performance by identifying for himself when he had learnt the words:

> *Well, I just, first, after a while when the trainer counted, I just thought I knew it, and then I repeated it at home, and, then when it came to the practice next day I checked if I got it right, and I did.*

In the next extract, a student explains learning tactics in sport. While he acknowledges he has learnt from others, he also identifies his own role in the learning process. Identifying one's own role in learning is an integral feature of a Category D conception of learning because understanding is related to knowledge of self. Through his explanation of how he learnt fair play and the tactics and rules of a game and then incorporated these into *manoeuvres*, this student demonstrated a more sophisticated view of learning than that involved in simply performing the task (Category C). He realised he had to translate all these rules and tactics in an intentional manner and with understanding in order to "beat the player" or "score a goal":

> S: *Yes, I like sport when I'm doing sport, and when I'm learning in sport, I learn about fair play and what the rules are of the sport, and you learn tactics all the time.*
> R: *What are tactics?*
> S: *They are things; they are actually moves that you can use or manoeuvres that you can use for, to try and beat the player or try and, you know, score a goal in soccer or something.*

R: Who teaches you tactics?

S: You actually basically teach yourself or you can just get, like, if you're watching TV, the professionals, you can get tactics off them, and you learn off the TV as well, because you're learning new tactics all the time.

The next extract provides another example, within the context of a speech competition, of a learning activity outside school in which a student demonstrates understanding rather than simply attempting to reproduce or memorise (Category B); or merely recite (Category C):

S: With poems, they give you a poem, so I have to read it over and over, and then you think how you're saying it. If you're saying it full on to the audience, and if it's narrative that means you're telling a story or you're just saying out words. So, if what you're saying is narrative, you've got to think how you're saying it. So I did another narrative, but that wasn't facing the audience. You were behind this box because it's for the Hearing Association Cup. So, like, something you're um ... you have to imagine yourself on the radio, you have to say it in a different voice.

R: How would it sound different?

S: You've got to project the words a bit more with, um ... assonance or something, and you've got to really say them out, not too loud, but so they hear. It's got to be really crisp; you've got to hear every word.

The students who held a conception of learning in Category D all alluded to the importance of a sense of purpose when learning, with goal setting being cited as one way of achieving personal direction and focus. As one explained:

If you don't set goals ... you don't really have any sort of ... you can't focus on what you have to do, and you just do it without thinking. If you have goals, you can plan what you're going to do and do it as best you can.

A Category D conception of learning also rests on the understanding that learning is a process that involves teaching others:

Learning means teaching yourself to do well and do better, preparing yourself for the future. It involves you teaching others as well, because you learn the skill and you can use it to teach others.

One student explained how he supported a peer who had difficulty understanding work in class; he provided support because he was able to understand the material. He explained that he often helped his peer and was "virtually a kid teacher".

Some students also recognised the importance of calling on peers to facilitate understanding of particular tasks, particularly when those peers could make sense of the material and turn it into "student-friendly" language. Students in this study frequently said that when they did not understand the teacher, their peers or siblings often described concepts in ways they could understand, as the following student explained:

> *First, I probably go and ask the teacher, and she'd write something up in my book, and I'd try and follow that. And then I'd ask my friends, like, they've already figured the skill because the teacher hasn't, like, she's the one who figured it, but she doesn't really use it at that time, so I ask them how they use it and what they've done to get the answer right, and they'll tell you, and then you just sit down and try to figure it out yourself.*

When this student said that she tried to "figure it out" herself, she was indicating the importance of *understanding* the material, after having it explained. So while her friends had already figured out the skill and had explained it to her, she realised she needed to understand it or figure it out herself to have learnt.

Students do not always rely on friends to help develop understanding through learning; they may also turn to siblings, as was the case with a student having problems learning the remote control functions for the television:

> *Well, my father taught me and my brother, but I wasn't too sure, so my brother helped me too. He taught me, he showed me which buttons to press on the remote. My father used big words which I didn't understand. My brother in his words was more my level, so he said, 'Well, you push this button, it's the channel button, so you press this one,' and my father might have said, 'Well this button is ... it changes the channel,' but my brother would've said it in a different way that I could understand it more.*

This example shows a student reacting to incomprehensible information and realising she needed some understanding of what she was learning in order to be ready to learn. When she felt comfortable about some aspect of the content, she could "listen and know more":

I would understand it a lot more. My brain shuts off when I, when it hasn't seen something before or, like, it's something new and it doesn't want to filter in information about it, and if I know a little bit about it, then I can listen and know more.

Different ways of knowing (E): How can I solve this problem?

The fifth category of learning, and the most sophisticated, was demonstrated by students who discussed learning as different ways of knowing. These students were interested in developing a greater awareness of multiple solutions to problems, a notion best explained by the student who said he learnt to see things "in different ways" and then related this learning to other subjects. While some learners, who conceptualised learning within Category D, other learners (i.e., those with a more sophisticated conception of learning in Category E), use that meaning in different ways across different subject areas. When this happens, learning for students is exciting and fun, and they thirst to learn for learning's sake.

Learners in this category no longer focus on finding the one correct answer or the one solution to a problem. Instead, they look at the possibilities associated with different ways of knowing and with seeing things in different ways. They are interested in finding connections, similarities and differences in what they are learning. As the following student discovered, there is more than one way to name a number. While, in mathematical terms, this action may simply be a matter of "renaming a number", it was, for the student, an understanding that led him to a new world within which to learn mathematics. His excitement was infectious:

> S: Well, then you have more time to get it into your brain, and you find it easier instead of trying to just fix it in one day. Well, then you can do it over; you learn one thing, and you can do it in different ways, not just learning one thing to do it that way.
> R: Okay, can you give me an example?
> S: Well, maybe doing fractions, and you learnt that three-tenths can also mean the same as .3 or .30 can also mean 30 over 100 and it can also mean 30 percent. Like, most people, if they don't really know, they'd see it as three-tenths could never be 30 percent. Just like one-quarter; 25 percent is like one-quarter. If you don't see that that way, then it's not really.
> R: How do you get to see it that way?

> S: Well, over time—well, you've got to know a quarter is something divided into four pieces. So if 100 was divided into four pieces you've got to see 25 and then it's 25 percent. But if you just think 'How on Earth could I get from 1 over 4 to 25 over 100?' and then you'd say, 'How would you get 4 into 100?' And then if you multiply 4 by 25, you'd get to 100, and you multiply 1 by 25 is 25.

Learners who hold this conception of learning realise they do not have to rely on having been taught something in order for them to learn. This conception is critical to the notion of a lifelong learner because it is as much about "knowing yourself" as it is about "learning something new", and it contrasts markedly with the earlier conceptions characterised by the type of thinking that says "teachers talk and students listen". In the following extract, learning is shown as an active process that takes place between the learner and the teacher, not as a function of the teacher talking. The student discusses going beyond "understanding", which is associated with Category D, to testing different ways of doing something:

> Oh no, it just helps you, but then you've got to help yourself by putting it in, and then you've got to practise by yourself in a corner or somewhere. You can't just say, 'Oh, well, now he's taught me I can do it.' You've got to keep writing things and testing different ways of doing it. Then that only happens because you understand it, and so understanding means that all the help that's brought in is making you confident to know what you're doing.

In the dialogue below, the student highlights the link between learning and understanding. His aim was to *understand* what he had learnt, rather than memorise or recall factual information. His conception of learning is generally within Category E because he recalls learning as a process of greater awareness and of having come to know something "thoroughly ... all of it, every single bit", which he can then link "to other subjects". The student's interest in seeing things in other ways, from different perspectives, is evident here, as is his awareness of relating his learning to "everything you do":

> R: Okay, so it's not just good enough for someone to tell you something, but you actually have to ...
> S: Understand it.
> R: Oh, you have to understand it?

S: *Yeah.*

R: *Where does understanding come into learning?*

S: *Well, once you reinforce it, well, then you start to see it in different ways, and then that happens, that only happens because you understand it, and so understanding means that all the help that's brought in is making you confident to know what you're doing.*

R: *Okay, can you tell me the difference between understanding and learning?*

S: *Well, learning is just knowing something and once you know it, if you know it thoroughly, you know all of it, every single bit, then you can relate it to other subjects and you can relate it to, um ... everything you do.*

Learners holding Category E conceptions of learning tend to realise that outside-the-classroom contexts also offer learning that takes account of various perspectives and viewpoints:

S: *I figure them out, um ... different ways, because when you, you've always got to see things at a different angle, like, if somebody's got in a fight, you look at both, you don't just look at one person.*

R: *Why's that?*

S: *Because everybody's got a different point of view, and they might want to lie or just get out of trouble. Because I have been a mediator before, so you have to listen to both different kinds of angles.*

Summary

The Year 7 students I interviewed held views of learning that grouped into five categories portraying a hierarchy of conceptions ranging from least sophisticated to most sophisticated (A to E). Conceptions in the lower range (A, B and C) showed learning as an external process of getting knowledge "into one's head" from "out there". The students who recognised learning in a more sophisticated way tended to see knowledge as being created by themselves *with* others; they viewed learning as "seeing something in a different way" (D and E). However, these students still recognised the importance of the earlier conceptions.

The interview transcripts frequently revealed students using the more sophisticated views of learning when describing out-of-school learning. The reason why seemed, in part, to be because the students understood that assessment systems require them to recognise and regurgitate public knowledge in exchange for grades and marks. Teachers need to understand how students conceptualise their learning in order to help them not only develop more sophisticated conceptions of learning (that is, seeing learning as "changing the way they see things" rather than "acquiring knowledge to fill up their brains") but also monitor their own learning through self-assessment. Students who view learning only as acquiring knowledge tend to monitor their learning differently from students who view learning as an attempt to see things in a different way.

Some of the learning strategies students described in this chapter (such as those relating to rote learning, memory and thinking) are strategies teachers can apply in the classroom. Encouraging students to use rote learning to develop their understanding and thinking about a concept helps them develop a strategy to learn and problem solve, and is therefore more useful for students than rote learning that has no purpose other than information recall. To solve problems, learners must be able to recall knowledge and information that *informs* the problem-solving process. Vygotsky considered the close relationship between memory and thinking particularly relevant to effort designed to encourage learners to take on a more sophisticated conception of learning and self-assessment:

> Memory in early childhood is one of the central psychological functions upon which all the other functions are built ... for the very young child to think means to remember; at no time after very early childhood do we see such a close connection between these two psychological functions. *For the young child, to think means to recall; but for the adolescent, to recall means to think.* Her memory is so 'logicalised' that remembering is reduced to establishing and finding logical relations; recognising consists in discovering that element which the task indicates has to be found. (Vygotsky, 1978, p. 50)

For many of the students who held the least sophisticated conceptions of learning (A and B), the notion of remembering was an end in itself, even though "remembering in everyday life is usually in the service of accomplishing some other goal rather than being itself the end for the activity" (Rogoff & Mistry, 1990, p. 206). Why did these students want to remember? So they could answer the test or teacher's questions the next day. This observation reiterates the important point that students' goal-setting activities are integral to the learning process, and that self-assessment of learning is critical for goal setting. How, then, do students self-assess? The next chapter explores theories and policies of assessment, while Chapter 6 outlines students' conceptions of self-assessment, and shows how students identify when they have learnt something.

CHAPTER 5

Assessment and self-assessment

> Perhaps the most critical need for students to meet their own future learning needs is their capacity to judge what their own learning needs are and how they go about meeting them. Self-assessment ability is therefore a critical ingredient for students' lifelong learning. (Tan, 2007, p. 125)

While learning is central to this book, a key part of the context for that learning is the various ways learners experience assessment, and the aspects of their learning they self-assess. Learning and assessment are thus inextricably linked (Black & Wiliam, 2006; Earl & Katz, 2008; Harlen, 2006): people do not just learn, they always learn "something" (Marton & Booth, 1996), but this learning is not always the something we can assess. The interplay between learning and assessment within the classroom often leads learners to believe that when they participate in assessment tasks, it is their learning that is being assessed. This is not so. No assessment tool can measure learning, just as a measuring cup cannot measure the amount of sun in the sky, which is why, in this chapter, I consider issues of assessment relative to learning. More specifically, I provide an overview of the effect of assessment on students and their learning, the impact of the political context of assessment on learning, assessment as a dividing practice, and sustainable assessment. In so doing, I focus on these questions: How does assessment influence learning? Why is self-assessment important to learning, and to assessment?

Assessment: Roles, functions, influence

Assessment serves different roles and functions, and while I discuss these briefly here, I am more interested in this chapter in focusing on experiences related to assessment and the implications of assessment than on what assessments *intend* or *purport* to do.

Previous scholarship has identified three broad functions of assessment practice in school-based settings: (1) support for learning, (2) the certification of individual students and (3) public accountability of teachers and institutions (Black, 1993). A fourth function, that of assessment as a change agent, is becoming increasingly evident (Wiliam, 2010). Black and Wiliam (2006) liken formative[3] assessment to a Trojan Horse when its application actively compels teachers to change their pedagogical practices, relationships with their students and communication with parents.

Assessment can thus be a double-edged sword for teachers. On the one hand, it can provide them with a powerful means of engaging with and reviewing *their own learning*, and subsequently reflecting and rethinking their own teaching and assessment practices (Kirkwood, 2007). On the other hand, it can become a punitive tool if the assessment data are publicised and used to create league tables (Black, 1998). In both Britain and the United States, attempts have been made to link the results of student assessments to performance-based pay for educators (Gleason, 2000).

These four functions influence teacher assessments in the classroom; in turn, these assessments influence student learning. Since the early 1990s, tensions have

---

3 While formative and summative assessment methods are both used in classrooms, they offer different functions and necessitate different relationships with the teacher (Black & Wiliam, 2006; Gipps, 1994). Summative assessment occurs at the end of an activity, module or term; it evaluates whether learning has occurred and is often associated with high-stakes testing. In contrast, formative assessment is ongoing; it assists with decisions about the teaching programme and is aimed at facilitating student learning. Gipps (1994) refers to "trickle up testing" (p. 13) to describe formative assessment that uses a wide range of activities to collect information about the learner and his or her learning. However, in practice, formative assessment is often used in a summative way—just think how many times a student is asked to self-assess work after a module or activity and to place a grade, smiley or other indicator of how they felt about their achievement.

been identified between assessment for learning and assessment for accountability (Nisbet, 1994), although, according to Black, Harrison, Lee, Marshall, and Wiliam (2003), teachers who use both summative and formative approaches to assessment can successfully use formative practice to support student preparation for summative assessment. Crooks (2006) argues that there is "little point in accountability processes if they do not have substantial formative effects alongside their summative purposes" (p. 14). As such, it could be viewed that, in general, the aim of assessment for learning (formative) is to show that we, as teachers, enable student learning (summative).

However, the accountability agenda has sharpened this edge in countries where students, and potentially schools, are assessed against age-related national standards in order to raise student achievement. This agenda creates an illusion that we can identify what is important, use a measuring tool and raise the bar. But, inevitably, teachers will focus on teaching what the standards establish as important, students will identify what should be remembered, achievement scores may increase, standards may rise, but neither learning nor understanding can be guaranteed.

The quest for measurement and for the data sets required to "measure learning" is not unique to teachers and schools. As Broadfoot (2000) argues, outcome data have become an intrusive reification of what is shown to be valued:

> We live in a world obsessed with data; with the collection and dissemination of performance indicators, statistics, measures, grades, marks and categories. In a world in which it is assumed that quality can be defined, compared and certified. And a world in which what cannot be perceived, explained and measured is deemed to be either unimportant or non-existent. (p. 199)

There has been much debate in education over whether learning, of the kind articulated in, for example, the newly introduced key competencies of *The New Zealand Curriculum* (Ministry of Education, 2007), *can* be assessed. If it can, then, as the argument has it, its outcomes must be identified and defined, be subject to observation and made public. Given that research shows we prioritise our teaching and learning based on what will be assessed, and that what we assess highlights what we value, any form of assessment requires careful consideration (Eisner, 2000).

In school-based settings, certain forms of "knowledge" lead to a type of assessment that determines what is "known"; classroom contexts still commonly utilise teachers' "known-answer quizzing" (Hodgen & Webb, 2008; Rogoff & Toma, 1997). Thus, we assess spelling, multiplication tables, science formulas or any situation where there is a common understanding of what is "right": two multiplied by two is always four, and Wellington has been the capital city of New Zealand since 1865. This form of assessment measures ways of knowing rather than the individual's learning. As Hodgen and Webb (2008) concluded after observing teachers using responsive questioning and evaluative listening, "… telling a student whether their response is correct provides almost no information about what they need to do to learn more" (p. 76). In similar vein, Nicholls and Hazzard (1993) point out that tests:

> cannot help teachers discern what a child understands about addition of two digit numbers, the nature of sentences, the source of rain, how to tell how long it will be until lunchtime, or any of the myriad topics that will come up in the next few days … Children's knowledge changes rapidly … the collation on paper of so much detailed information by the teacher would leave little time and energy for the process of education. This psychometric enterprise has nothing to do with the delicate, idiosyncratic, evolving, forward looking, creative process of teaching. (p. 42)

Because ideas about what should be learnt, what is learnt and what learning is legitimate and valued are mediated by different cultural and social values, school based assessment systems measure specific learning outcomes, which, for many countries, are linked to predetermined standards. These outcomes become what teachers and students value, or at least what they focus on, as they strive to succeed within the school-based system. While we know outcomes can be identified through particular assessment measures, and that students can be given a test score, grade or level of achievement, there is considerable disagreement about whether we are measuring learning or an outcome of that learning. If we assume certain forms of knowledge, and even understanding, can be assessed formally and informally, then our assessment systems invariably assess these forms of learning. If, however, we recognise certain intangible kinds of learning—for example, how to describe the sunset, how a child imagines building a spaceship, how a young child creates a visual image of a washing basket in the sun—then how might we talk about this learning? The answer depends on one's views about learning and knowledge, and this determines what is to be assessed.

In schools, where assessment takes place alongside teaching practices on a daily basis, learners' and teachers' day-to-day actions and their learning are continually influenced by how and why these assessments are undertaken. Some forms of assessment remain invisible to learners, but all forms of assessment send messages to learners that build on, or challenge, aspects of their respective identities. Teachers' messages about assessment can have a particularly marked influence on learners; some have unintended consequences. Maintaining a focus on teachers and their teaching is therefore an important consideration during any discussion of assessment.

As Campbell (2003) identifies in *The Ethical Teacher*, "often instantaneous, seemingly involuntary, the actions and reactions of teachers send subtle messages to students about how they are thought of as people, not simply learners" (p. 28). In *Culture Speaks*, Bishop and Berryman (2006) report the voices of Māori learners within secondary schools who gave powerful messages that teachers needed *to care*—about them as individuals, and about them as Māori. Even those students identified as "nonengaged" reported that they wanted to learn. If learners are embraced in this way, by their teachers, then these students' learning outcomes can be celebrated through careful, systematic and purposeful assessment processes that involve learners as observers of their own learning.

For this to occur, the assessor's knowledge and power must be shared with the learner. Ultimately, the most powerful form of *understanding learning* is self-assessment, and the only person who can truly assess learning is the individual—the learner. Therefore, self-assessment aligned with knowing one's own conception of learning is central to this process. Measurement has little role to play in any exploration of learning relative to self-assessment. Even formative assessment strategies, where assessment is integral to the learning process, have little to offer learners in respect of developing metacognitive or cognitive strategies that they can use in different learning contexts.

Assessment: The political context

Empirical evidence shows that "most students try to deliver what they predict the teachers will reward" (Ramsden, 1988, p. 21), that assessment is a key factor affecting motivation and that students who receive higher grades perceive the system as fairer than those who receive lower grades (Harlen, 2006). These experiences for learners take place within the wider political context of that assessment.

Educational reform within countries such as France, Germany, the Netherlands, Spain, Sweden, Britain, the United States and New Zealand has, for years, focused on assessment as a cornerstone for change. In the early 1990s, the rationale of "raising national standards" underpinned much of the reform, but this took two directions— assessment for accountability, and assessment for enhancing learning (Black, 1998; Nisbet, 1993, 1994). Depending on whether the assessment methods employed are used to meet the aim of accountability or learning, the reporting of results can lead into rounds of reform that make little difference to student learning (Black, 1998). One example will suffice here. The OECD Programme for International Student Assessment (PISA) produces cross-national comparisons based on the students' results from the participating countries, including New Zealand. PISA surveys the literacy (reading, mathematical and scientific) achievement of 15-year-olds every three years. Each country reportedly uses its PISA data to monitor *student learning*, but the release of this information by the OECD, and its subsequent reporting in the media and via government agencies, tends to result in "country league tables" that allow comparison of students' scores both "within country" and "between country". For example:

> Finland, with an average of 563 score points, was the highest-performing country on the PISA 2006 science scale. Six other high-scoring countries had mean scores of 530 to 542 points: Canada, Japan and New Zealand and the partner countries/economies Hong Kong–China, Chinese Taipei and Estonia.
>
> On average across OECD countries, 1.3% of 15-year-olds reached Level 6 of the PISA 2006 science scale, the highest proficiency level. These students could consistently identify, explain and apply scientific knowledge, and knowledge about science, in a variety of complex life situations. In New Zealand and Finland this figure was at least 3.9%, three times the OECD average. (OECD, 2006)

The 2006 PISA results showed that, overall, New Zealand students performed well relative to the international average score in science literacy, despite the large number of New Zealand students scoring well below the New Zealand average. Poor performance on the test correlated very strongly, in all of the participating countries, with low SES. For example, in New Zealand, the students who achieved less well were disproportionately represented by Māori and Pasifika students, who also tend to be disproportionately represented in the lower socioeconomic brackets: "New Zealand has one of the largest spreads of student achievement, and *achievement is more closely correlated with students' socio-economic status than in many OECD countries*" (New Zealand Treasury, 2008, emphasis added).

Although it seems that we cannot ignore or "reframe" socioeconomic variables as educational ones, New Zealand entered a round of educational change intent on raising standards rather than addressing issues such as poverty. In late 2008, New Zealand's newly elected National Government renewed the emphasis on using assessment to "raise standards" by passing the Education (National Standards) Amendment Act 2008. The legislation required primary schools to compare the progress of their students against national standards in literacy and numeracy that would be developed in 2009. The lack, at the time, of national standards against which to assess students, and little else, apart from international comparisons, to confirm that students were not achieving to some supposed standard, reinforce the notion of government using assessment as a means of hiding "unpalatable truths" underlying student underachievement. As Graham (2008) points out, "the problem for educators is when the goal of policy becomes to improve rankings on … league tables rather than to improve the quality of education in our schools" (p. 22). This eventuality tends to put increased pressure on teachers to teach to the test or show increased student achievement (Au, 2009; Bullough, 2008).

Part of this pressure comes from the increased "performativity" culture infiltrating teacher practice, where "public measures of school performance" influence what teachers do, and why (Daugherty & Ecclestone, 2006, p. 166). Bullough (2008), writing with reference to the United States, argues that "there appears to be an almost exclusive focus among policymakers on increasing student learning, in the form of achieving prescribed learning 'outcomes', to the neglect of teacher well-being—and probably, ultimately, even to the neglect of the wellbeing of children" (p. 20). Even resurgent efforts to look at alternative forms of assessment, such as rubrics (Andrade, 2000) and learning records (Barr, 2000), often locate these in a policy "outcomes" agenda. As Bruner (1996) argues, assessment focused on raising standards often occurs at the expense of looking more carefully at the core function of the classroom, namely learning and teaching.

Assessment as a dividing practice

For teachers, making decisions about assessment and knowing why these decisions are made are important teaching processes because, as I have already emphasised in this chapter, the resultant practices ultimately affect student learning. The fact that some assessments can isolate certain learners from the learning process (Au, 2009; Broadfoot, 1996) is demonstrated in the choice of whether to use "student centred, multi-cultural, and portfolio assessments, or to use teacher centred tests or standardised exams in which women and minorities have traditionally scored lower than men and whites" (Shor, 1992, p. 15). Rosner (2003) suggests that the latter approach can be viewed as "psychometrically reinforced racism" (p. 24), while Au (2009) claims that "standardized tests … with their focus on individual, meritocratic achievement, serve a particular ideological purpose within the (re)production of socioeconomic inequalities" (p. 46). When making decisions about assessment, our main concern, according to Nisbet (1994), should reside with "the group with least power, the learners. In designing the future pattern of assessment, the prime consideration should be the effect on learning, and decisions about assessment should be made as close as possible to the learners" (p. 168).

Recent educational assessment history shows that formative assessment, from the late 1990s, has done exactly what Nisbet called for, identified ways to increase student involvement in assessment *for their own* learning. However, I consider that the influence of those assessment advances, especially in terms of the teacher–student relationship, has not fully captured the spirit of being concerned with the interests of learners. Let me offer a promising example of an initiative that has captured that spirit. Stevenson (2008) showed that when students had opportunity to identify their own learning goals and then connect them, through Web 2.0 technology, with "experts" able to offer advice and information related to the students' areas of interest, the students began setting their own increasingly sophisticated learning goals within the classroom and without reference to a formal assessment system:

> I had seen in the online work with mentors that when students chose goals for themselves, they were significantly higher than the goals which may have been expected by the teacher or by an NCEA [National Certificate of Educational Achievement] achievement standard. Consequently the students, as part of a real life artist community were now 'going for gold'—getting past the idea of NCEA and instead looking at real world performance and excellence. (Stevenson, 2008, p. 135)

This is the outcome of assessment that we need to aim for. But when seeking the positive, we need to remain mindful of the negative, because when we know what we do not want to do, we have a better notion of what we do want to do. Since his seminal review of classroom evaluation practices, Crooks (1988) has continued to stress (e.g., Crooks, 2006, 2007) the need to avoid assessment practices that encourage students to approach learning superficially—to "learn to the test". When assessment practices are such that they inhibit or suppress student learning (Ecclestone, 2007; James, 2006), they can become dividing practices (Foucault, 1977), because in essence they create arbitrary distinctions between winners and losers (Hanson, 1993). Students in school settings know this. When asked to identify the point of tests and exams, one 16-year-old secondary school student responded:

> To get the winners and the losers. You know, to help create a margin between people who pass and the people who fail. So that employers know this person is better than this person, so we'll take him. [R: So it's got nothing to do with your own personal learning? It's to do with employers?] Yeah, they [the teacher] say you've got to work at your own pace and stuff. But really that's not how society works. You know if you're not as good as the other people then the other people are going to get employment and not you. When you're an adult if you're unemployed and not doing much, I can't really call them losers or anything. They just ... yeah, if someone has got a nice job because he has a good education, then he would be considered a winner. And if someone who had the same amount of brains but, or maybe not the same amount of brains, but didn't do well at school and is unemployed, then he's a loser ... I want to be a winner. (Bourke, 1996, p. 8)

Research continues to show that the ease with which control processes, such as tests and examinations, can be systematised encourages the ongoing legitimisation of learning as static and individual. Tests and examinations, says Kvale (2007), "control what and how students learn" (p. 63), and over time, these processes give students messages about "what is worth learning". However, as my own earlier research indicates (Bourke, 1996), many students recognise and are critical of assessment that they consider serves institutionalised ends. In the following extract from an interview, a 17-year-old describes the dilemma of wanting to answer exam questions in the way *he* sees fit but knowing that he needs to work towards the *preferred* way of seeing the world. For him, assessment is the "end" as defined by the system, rather than a "means" to support his own learning:

> Basically, we've got to learn to pass the exams. Like the teachers in English; we learn stuff for the exams, there might be another way, a better way of doing something, you don't worry about it. It's done this way so you get the marks. If you don't do it this way, you don't get the marks. You might have lots of knowledge about something—about biology, right? You've learnt about the liver and how the body functions and stuff like that. You become a real expert in it, but they're not studying that in the exam. But the teachers always give you guidelines in what to study. It's like poetry. Someone or not someone—man—has sort of made a way that says, 'This is nice poetry and this poetry is garbage.' And who is to say this poetry is garbage and this poetry is good poetry? Basically, you have got to have the right answer. Like, you might think the garbage is nice poetry, but if you write that down in the exam, you don't get the marks. (Bourke, 1996, p. 10)

Tom Greene, a student in England about to receive his A level results, made similar points when he wrote to *The Independent* (17 August 2006), questioning the examination and assessment process:

> Exam preparation, and increasingly education, is now about adapting to this system; forcing an examiner, wearily red-penning through piles of paper, to give you that top grade. Students are drilled to jump through hoops that the examiner is holding …
>
> Today's results will represent a year of mechanised working towards four grades, four grades that will be added to another year's work of retakes and preparation

to produce ... another three/four grades. Isn't it about time that grades were for life—not just for August?

Hanson (1993) would agree with the summations of these two young men: "In a very real sense, tests have invented all of us. They play an important role in determining what opportunities are offered to or withheld from us, they mould the expectations and evaluations that others form of us, and they heavily influence our assessments of our own abilities and worth" (p. 4). Crooks (1988) and James (2006) also point out the demotivating effect tests can have on learners when they "fail" them and/or when they believe there is only one "correct" answer. A study in Northern Ireland, involving 16-year-olds, showed these students focusing only on what was needed to "pass" their examinations (Harlen, 2008).

But when discussing how they assess their work in relation to outside-school activities, such as cricket, music and hobbies, students often identify intrinsic ends; they are not necessarily motivated by external rewards, nor do they require external sources to structure and acknowledge their success (Bourke, 2000). The 17-year-old student quoted above who described learning as a process required to pass exams later referred to his work in a supermarket where he said he could be creative and innovative and was rewarded for this. In this setting, he had greater ownership of the assessment of his performance because that assessment gave him information (feedback) about behaviours and actions that he valued because they made, for him, sense within the context of his life.

Self-assessment and lifelong learning: Sustainable assessment

Students need, and many want, to be prepared for the rest of their lives and equipped to learn and assess when there is no teacher around. As student Tom Greene (quoted in the previous section) stated, learning should be for life, "not just for August". Even when learners do well within the structured learning environment of a school-based setting, they may not be particularly effective as *lifelong* learners because the learning pathway is less directed (Deakin Crick, Broadfoot, & Claxton, 2004). In Deakin Crick et al.'s view, *strategic awareness* is a necessary and critical component of successful lifelong learning and needs to be encouraged and taught:

"the need to *teach* students the skills of self-assessment and target-setting" (p. 266) means learners must be encouraged to articulate their learning intentions and their thoughts and feelings about a learning task. In a future-focused lifelong learning environment, teaching how to assess is potentially more important than assessing learning outcomes. Self-assessment is pivotal to such a process.

Every learner's life includes some "thing" they can self-assess. Often, the type of learning (a part of living) most easily assessed by children arises from out-of-school activities because these are the events that formal systems rarely assess and reward: stars, stamps, grades and stickers are not the currency of most out-of-school informal learning activities. When a child learns to tie her shoelaces, brush her hair, clean her teeth, dress herself, rollerblade or ride a bike, she reaches a stage of saying, "I can do this myself." The hair may still be dishevelled, the teeth not entirely cleaned and the trainer wheels still on the bike, but all children understand when they can determine they have achieved *their* learning. It is not just the observable action but also the inherent feeling of "doing" and experiencing the success of the activity. They start to see their actions and *themselves* in a different way; they are learning, and they continue to set themselves new learning goals.

In contrast, in school-based settings, certain external markers herald the arrival of new learning. From an early age, children receive stars, stamps, stickers or exclamations of "Well done!" In today's formative assessment milieu, their teachers may also give them specific feedback and feedforward to support further learning. However, in a school-based setting, not all students can rely on themselves to know that they have learnt; that is, not all students can satisfactorily self-assess their own learning and understanding in relation to an activity. Self-assessment includes the ability to understand what constitutes the actual task, activity or learning event, as well as the ability to recognise one's own knowledge in relation to this task and to recognise how others' knowledge and skills can support this process. It is these aspects of learning that are essential to tools such as the personal education plan.

Along with profiling, records of achievements, learning stories, narrative assessment, portfolios and projects, self-assessment contributes to the philosophy of including the learner in the assessment and learning processes. The aim of incorporating self-assessment into the evaluation of student learning is to encourage independent learners, and to develop metacognitive strategies. As Stipek, Recchia, and McClintic (1992) point out, self-assessment is "undoubtedly one of the most important milestones in children's development" (p. 1). Earl and Katz (2008), amongst many others, highlight the importance of self-assessment in relation to self-monitoring. Research shows that students who engage in self-assessment typically find meaning and relevance in their learning, which leads to an increase in their motivation to learn and their engagement with the learning activity (Harlen, 2006). Self-assessment is also a powerful tool for teachers. Klenwoski, Askew, and Carnell (2006), for example, found that teachers who successfully use assessment strategies such as portfolios, based on a guided participation in practice or apprenticeship model, develop their understanding of their own learning.

The self-assessment process has several important features:
- It allows learners to establish their own goals in relation to the identified task.
- It helps learners understand the teachers' standards or criteria or both and how and why to apply these to their work.
- It encourages learners to identify their own standards and criteria and actively use these.
- It allows learners to judge the extent to which they have met their own and others' standards and criteria.

These features allow scaffolding of independent learning and give teachers the means of learning more about the learner. Although, as Tan (2007) reminds us, self-assessment is essentially a tool that learners can use to identify and evaluate their own performance outside of "formal study", learners can nonetheless use it within school-based contexts. In his study involving students in a higher education setting, Tan (2007) identified three forms of self-assessment: programme-driven self-assessment, teacher-driven self-assessment and future-driven self-assessment. From the findings of his study, Tan deemed the third form the one best suited to harnessing students' own capacity to make informed decisions and "focus beyond the expectations of the teacher and the programme of study" (p. 120). As one of the students in Tan's study said, "Because it is professionally imperative for nurses, for doctors, for teachers, for everybody, that you're able to realistically self-assess ... that *ability to self-assess is the springboard for your lifelong learning*" (p. 120, emphasis in original).

In some cases, teachers can facilitate learners' understanding and use of their knowledge by making explicit the criteria for assessment in relation to performance goals. However, this approach has the danger of hindering students' self-identification of their progress because it offers them the temptation of focusing only on the absolute "correct" or "incorrect" aspects of the assessment. There is also potential for others to hinder children's self-assessment, as in some cases "children's self-evaluations are to a large extent a reflection of significant others' evaluations, i.e., parents, teachers and peers" (Gipps & Tunstall, 1998, p. 150).

Stipek et al. (1992) explored the emotional self-evaluations and reactions of one- to five-year-olds in achievement- or outcome-based contexts. They also looked at whether adult evaluations, expressed as praise, influenced the way the child self-assessed. Their conclusion was that while adult feedback affected learners' assessments of their self-worth (as linked to notions of rejection and acceptance), it had less impact on the children's self-assessment of their performance level.

Incorporating self-assessment in teaching and learning

Research shows that self-assessing learners become better able to self-regulate further learning and to develop a greater sense of control over their learning. They also are more likely than those who do not self-assess to accept responsibility for their learning, develop reflective thinking skills and apply metacognitive strategies. When teachers use self-assessment practices in classrooms, the outcomes tend to be improved student motivation and student engagement (Broadfoot, 1979; Kusnic & Finley, 1993) and, from there, increased student achievement (Ross & Starling, 2008). Intentional learning can occur if the students know what they *do not know*; self-assessment provides them with the means of establishing the boundary between knowing and not knowing.

The teacher–student relationship changes when teachers purposefully facilitate student self-assessment in their classrooms. The traditional role of the teacher is challenged, because teachers have to share their power in the learning and assessment processes with their students. Self-assessment demystifies the assessment process for learners because the criteria for assessment are made explicit; often, that explication is initiated by the learner. Teachers therefore need to be confident in releasing some of their traditional power, but in doing so, they still need to demonstrate what Onora O'Neill (2002) calls "intelligent accountability" for their students' learning. Linn (2003, 2004) and Crooks (2006, 2007) further developed this notion. Linn (2003) argued that this form of "accountability must entail broadly shared responsibility" (p. 3) between and among educators, students, administrators, policy makers, parents and researchers. Crooks (2006, 2007) proposed six criteria for intelligent accountability—criteria that usefully remind us of what is important in an era of accountability for learning and, most pressingly, in maintaining integrity of the "worth" of learning. Intelligent accountability, then, for Crooks (2006, pp. 7–12):

- preserves and enhances trust among the key participants
- involves participants in the process, offering them a strong sense of professional responsibility
- encourages deep, worthwhile responses rather than surface window dressing
- recognises and attempts to compensate for the severe limitations of our ability to capture educational quality in performance indicators
- provides a well-founded and effective feedback that promotes insight into performance and supports good decision making
- encourages participants to be more enthusiastic and motivated in their work.

Other types of intelligence, described by Perkins (1995) and further commented on by Broadfoot (2000), also have direct relevance for self-assessment. Perkins (1995) posits three kinds:

- fixed neurological intelligence, which Broadfoot (2000) claims can be measured through psychometric tests to obtain a static IQ score
- special*ized* and special*ist* knowledge, both tested through formal means and both of which we develop through experience over time
- reflective intelligence.

The last, according to Broadfoot (2000), can best be summarised as self-assessment, given that it encompasses "the ability to engage in the metacognitive monitoring of one's own learning that is likely to be the central feature of successful learning in the future" (p. 212). While reflective intelligence focuses on knowing oneself, it also emphasises understanding and self-assessment as an intentional metacognitive strategy. Having a strong sense of self, both personally and professionally, is pivotal to being a successful lifelong learner.

Summary

If we want to emphasise student learning and increase students' engagement in their own learning, we must place learners centre stage and support them to focus on their learning. Students need to experience assessment methods in ways dramatically different from those we currently employ; that is, they need to view assessment as a *tool for understanding their learning* rather than an assessment of, or for, their learning.

Assessment thus becomes the learner's mirror for this observation, to identify the form, shape, stage and function of their learning and their role in it—a mirror that neither distorts reality nor creates a negative harmful image of the learner. Young people should see their reflection of their own learning, and enhance their own self-worth and identity as part of this. They should see themselves learning in multiple contexts, in different ways and portraying different "selves" in much the same way as a chameleon displays different colours.

Assessment is a form of celebrating learning and giving learners positive, encouraging messages that their efforts are contributing to their own growth as an individual. When the assessment process enables learners to see their own identity valued and allows opportunities to showcase learning, learners find the process of assessment more meaningful. In contrast, assessments not relevant or meaningful to the learner generate an image they neither care for nor consider useful for enhancing further learning.

The New Zealand Curriculum's (Ministry of Education, 2007) key competencies are intended to support teachers and learners in building this knowledge. Thinking, using language, symbols and texts, managing self, relating to others and participating and contributing are vital skills for learners involved in self-assessment in multiple contexts. However, questions inevitably arise about the competencies when considered in the context of assessment. For example, who determines whether a learner is participating and contributing? Is a child looking out a window in a busy classroom contributing? Is a child creating difficulties for the teacher by behaving in ways that limit her own and others' contributions to learning and, if so, how? How do teachers get an overall sense of how the student is "managing self" across the multiple contexts of a learner's schooling? Would the child who misbehaves in a mathematics class in order to avoid a PE class be seen as "managing self"? The child who acts this way to avoid PE would no doubt say yes; the mathematics teacher would probably say no.

The answers are within the learner; the analysis within both teacher and learner. Therefore, we must understand learners' motivations for their actions because their goals for that action ultimately lead to the outcomes observed by teachers. The next chapter provides examples of students' conceptions of self-assessment; that is, how they know when they have learnt.

CHAPTER 6

How do students know when they have learnt?

*I actually know I've learnt it, like, I don't know why,
I just know I've learnt it. I think it's the way I feel.
It's just like that bit's fulfilled in my head—it's just a feeling.*

Like the young boy above, we all know how it feels to do something, long before anyone has confirmed the degree of achievement or has provided an external symbol of success. Grades, marks, congratulations or awards are all forms of acknowledgement that often confirm what we already know. We just *know*. We know this in the same way we know when we do not do so well on something, when we mess up, muck it up or move away from what we intended to do. But this knowledge is more than a feeling. Self-assessment is a learning focus that compels us to forge ahead, striving to attain our goals.

In short, self-assessment *is* learning, and because it is, it is a powerful strategy for personalising learning. In turn, it becomes a sense of fulfilment that feeds back to motivate us towards new learning and new goals. Therefore, self-assessment is more than just feeling good; it is a deliberate, intentional drive by the learner to calculate the task to be completed, the learning focus needed and the current knowledge that contributes to the goal. It is not possible to self-assess without knowledge of ourselves—that is, of our own identity. Because identity is formed in relationship to others, self-assessment is a social process.

From the learner's perspective, then, self-assessment is about "knowing" oneself in relation to one's own learning. Self-assessment is so inherently bound to what students think learning is and what they do when they learn that, as an assessment tool, it is largely redundant. In other words, the self-assessment takes place during learning, as a result of the learning and as a goal for that learning.

The New Zealand Curriculum (Ministry of Education, 2007) states that evidence of student learning is often "of the moment" and that "analysis and interpretation often takes place in the mind of the teacher, who then uses the insights gained to shape their actions as they continue to work with their students" (p. 39). What the curriculum document does not state is that much of the analysis and interpretation of learning is, for students, *in their minds*, and it is their interpretation of assessment data that contributes to the "engaged learner". Therefore, self-assessment is more usefully thought of as a process to "access" ourselves in relation to learning, than as an assessment of that learning. This chapter explores one key question: What are Year 7 students' conceptions of self-assessment?

Recently, Joy Cowley, an influential New Zealand children's author, was asked, "What is your key message for all aspiring or yet-unpublished authors?" Her written response highlights the importance of self-assessment:

1. Hang in there! It can be a long apprenticeship but it's worth it. Just remember that we all start in the same place.
2. Write something every day. Writing is like swimming. A coach won't be able to teach you much unless you are in the water and active.
3. It really helps if you are a good reader. You will become a better evaluator of your own work.
4. Share your writing with friends. I think it's important that we do this on the way to publication. Some folk say they just write for themselves but I find that hard to understand. Writing is a form of communication.
5. Write what you know. If the story isn't real to you, it won't be real to the reader. (Cowley, 2008)

Cowley provides very important messages about doing something of value to the learner—hang in there, keep going, evaluate your own work, share your work and keep it real. In this chapter, learners who hold more sophisticated conceptions of self-assessment illustrate how these messages make sense for them. They, too, place high emphasis on valuing their own work and talk about the motivation behind their goals.

Studying students' conceptions of self-assessment

The 26 students (15 males and 11 females) described in this chapter were in Year 7 at an intermediate school. Their ages ranged from 10.3 years to 12.3 years. The details of the phenomenographic approach that I took when interviewing the students and analysing the transcripts of those interviews are explained in Chapter 3. In this present chapter, I offer six distinct categories outlining the students' conceptions of self-assessment. I describe each category and use students' words to illustrate the meaning behind the conceptions. As was the case with the categories of learning presented in Chapter 4, the categories move from the least sophisticated to the most sophisticated and inclusive conceptions of self-assessment.

The categories outlined in the panel below show that the students who participated in my study had various understandings of how to self-assess their learning. The conceptions of self-assessment range from the two least sophisticated categories, where students relied on guidance and support from other people (Category A) and sources such as grades (Category B), to the more sophisticated understanding of self-assessment where students used their own performance (Category C) or pre-established criteria (Category D) to self-assess their learning. The most sophisticated conceptions of self-assessment involved students actively setting their own learning goals then self-assessing these (Category E), and establishing whether they valued the learning content enough to persevere with learning (Category F). A common question representing the students' views is included with each conception. For example, the least sophisticated conception of self-assessment (A) poses the hypothetical question, "Have I learnt?", while the common question for the most sophisticated category of self-assessment (F) is, "Is this worth learning?"

Students' conceptions of self-assessment	
A. Seeking an opinion	Self-assessment is receiving an opinion from an "expert". Students depend on others to confirm that learning has occurred. Teachers and parents are the predominant source of confirmation. This category is characterised by the question: *Have I learnt?*
B. Getting marks and grades	Self-assessment depends on a symbol (grade, star, stamp, sticker) to confirm learning. For students, these marks and grades identify how well they have learnt in relation to peers. This category is characterised by the question: *How much have I learnt?*
C. Performing	Self-assessment is viewed as the ability to perform a task. Students use the ability to perform or complete a task as an indicator of learning. They use peers and adults to model the desired performance in order to assess own performance. This category is characterised by the question: *What did I learn?*
D. Using criteria	Self-assessment involves the use of pre-established criteria to indicate learning. Students are most likely to view teaching their peers as an indicator of their own learning. Generally, these students believe their learning will improve. This category is characterised by the question: *Do I understand what I have learnt?*

E. Setting learning goals	Self-assessment is based on setting learning goals. Students are able to set criteria and goals and can evaluate tasks before assessing their own learning in relation to their goals. Students individually self-assess their own learning and use grades as benchmarks for monitoring performance. This category is characterised by the question: *What do I want to learn?*
F. Evaluating learning content	Self-assessment is part of determining the worth of the learning. Students consider the value of the content and the learning goal before assessing their own learning. They are prepared to persevere with learning if they consider the learning important and valuable. This category is characterised by the question: *Is this worth learning?*

There was a distinct difference between students who depended on external sources to confirm learning for their self-assessments (Categories A and B) and students who used external sources to verify, confirm or contribute to their own awareness of learning (Categories C, D, E, F). The students used external sources such as grades in different ways. Those with less confidence in self-assessing their work placed greater reliance on grades, whereas those more confident in their own ability to self-assess used grades either as confirmation of learning or in more competitive ways. For example, one boy did not assist other students in case they got a better grade than he did, and another said his friends laugh when they beat each other in a test. Some students also attributed high grades to getting into more elite groups in some curriculum areas; for example, mathematics.

Sometimes, the grades students assign to themselves through a self-assessment activity do not indicate how they truly perceive their work, nor do they demonstrate an awareness of their learning. Instead, when students are asked by their teacher to self-assess their own work in school by giving themselves a mark or grade, they do so for other reasons. They approach this task differently from the competitive way they exchange grade information with their peers. While it is favourable to get a good score from the teacher, it is not considered appropriate to give yourself a good grade. In the students' terms, giving yourself an average grade is appropriate, but allocating a low grade indicates you're putting yourself down while a high grade indicates you're skiting.

When considering learning in school settings and out-of-school settings, the students were more likely to say they relied on or used external forms of feedback in the former than in the latter. It was also apparent from the students' comments that they were generally more resourceful and independent and more confident in their abilities to identify and self-assess their learning when engaged in learning activities outside the school. The reason for this difference may be because out-of-school settings, whether involving activities in the community or school-related learning in out-of-school contexts, tend to be more performance based, with other people actively involved in the same or similar activities. Having peers and adults who can model the appropriate learning outcomes and having opportunity to participate in the activity increase students' opportunities to observe others and to self-assess their own and others' performances.

Seeking an opinion (A): Have I learnt?

Students with the least sophisticated conception of learning viewed self-assessment as primarily involving others. Self-assessment was a process of being told they had learnt:

> *It's, like, she [teacher] just says, 'Good work,' and she just writes a comment there. So you can just, like, know. Or else, if she says, like, 'Oh, you're not supposed to do this,' and you just, like, know … it's wrong.*

> *The teacher tells you if it's right or not.*

Learners holding this conception of self-assessment generally seek *confirmation* of learning from other people to identify or self-assess that they have learnt. The feedback they look for typically comes from teachers and parents. According to these students, this is, in fact, the purpose of the feedback—simply to tell them they have learnt. These students express a need to know *whether* they have learnt rather than *what* or *how much* they have learnt.

Although the students who held a conception of self-assessment in Category A reported taking part in self-evaluations or self-assessments in the classroom, they doubted the validity of their evaluations and required the teacher to confirm the "correct" evaluation. As one student stated, "My evaluation is sort of a guess; I don't know what the others' are" [other students' self-assessments]. Another boy said, "We want another opinion to see if we're doing all right because we can't really just tell by ourselves; we need someone else to ask or something." The students had little confidence in their own ability to evaluate even in more performance-based curriculum areas in a school setting, such as physical education (PE). When speaking about PE, one student noted, "When there's self-evaluation, kind of, like, that's by yourself, and you don't really know if it's right or not." The belief that student evaluation is not relevant was evident in such statements as "We usually compare the teacher's grades because he's the one that knows really how good it is."

When I asked students why the teacher's evaluation was so important, their responses reflected their belief that teachers knew the correct answer, and therefore could be relied on to guide and support self-assessment. The following thinking was typical:

> S: Because she'd set me something to do and she'd know the answer to it, and if I get the right answer, she'd know that I was learning.
> R: Oh I see. So she would know before you did?
> S: Well, I know that I was on the way to nearly learning it, and I wouldn't be sure if that was all that I had to learn for it or if there was more to learn about it, then she'd tell me.

This extract highlights not only the teacher's role in confirming learning but also the students' belief that the teacher is aware of their learning before they are.

The same student also demonstrated this thinking when he referred to out-of-school settings within the community. Having explained that he made picture frames for friends and relatives as well as to sell in the market, he said he relied on his parents to confirm whether he had learnt to produce a good product:

S: Well, in some of the things, in some of the picture frames I've made, um ... she's [mum], like ... she's, like, told me what to do, and I went away and did it and put it on my picture frame, like, told me where to put the moss and where to put the dried flowers and all that. And so I went away and did it. I wasn't sure about it, and you know I wasn't sure if that looked, that was all right, and if I could sell it properly, and she would tell me that that looks really good and that would be ... you know, good for selling and stuff.

R: So, for you, when you're designing something who decides?

S: Um ... either dad or mum usually, or sometimes me. Sometimes dad and mum may not be there, and I might just think it through and do it myself real good.

R: How would you feel then?

S: Well ... when I'm sure it's real good, I'd feel proud that I've done it, and so, but I usually check out with dad or mum—ask them if they like it and if they'd like one themselves.

Throughout the interview, whenever this student referred to the various crafts he made, he said he checked what he done with either his mother or father. Even in examples of work he completed at school through technicraft, he sought the opinion of his father. When he states in the following extract that his father told him "it looks really, really good", the student is identifying that he knows learning has occurred:

R: Okay, so how do you know what grade to give yourself?

S: Um, well, I don't usually give myself, I usually ask someone else to do it, because if I do it myself, I might think it's real good, but someone else might not, so I usually ask my dad and ask him if it's good, and he'll tell me if it's really good, what it's like. Like, I made a boomerang the other day at school and, um, he liked it, and he said, 'Yup, it looks really, really good.'

All students within this first category of self-assessment initially wanted to know whether they had learnt something. It is the first form of feedback a learner uses to self-assess, and is considered neither quantitative nor comparative. At this stage, it is not important to them to know how they performed in relation to others. However, once learners are comfortable with knowing they can achieve, they become interested in more quantitative measures—how much, how fast, what level, what group, what grade. This knowledge characterises the next stage (Category B).

Getting marks and grades (B): How much have I learnt?

As with the first category, teacher appraisal or some other form of external confirmation of learning dominate the learner's conception. However, Category B differs from A in that learners seek some *quantitative* or *relative* measure of their performance. Students' conceptualisations of self-assessment within Category B in my study looked to grades and marks for two purposes—knowing *that* they had learnt, and knowing *how much* they had learnt. In this view of self-assessment, learners need confirmation of learning through what they consider objective sources, such as marks or grades. They use this information to compare their learning with their previous performances, and in relation to the performance of other students. They use pre- and post-test results to "measure" their progress, even though the scores they attain hold little relevance to *what* they learn:

> *I only learnt a little bit because I only got 54 percent. I think I got 54 percent on the first test and something like 65 percent or something on the second, so it's not that much.*

This category represents a more sophisticated category of self-assessment than Category A because learners have moved from wanting to know whether they have learnt, to wanting to know "by how much" they have learnt. In both categories, the learners rely on the guidance and expertise of some other person, but with B, they are interested in putting some indicator of quantity on the learning. They see tests and other forms of assessment as being designed to help the teacher know what they have learnt, and in some cases to communicate this knowledge to the student. As these students in my study noted:

> *Tests tell you what you need to improve on. Marks tell myself what I've got to improve on.*

> *[Tests] declare what age you're at, if you know that you've learnt.*

When these learners are not given the results, they assume the teacher uses this knowledge to develop the teaching programme, as these two students explained:

> *[Tests are] for the teachers to find out what you already know about the subject and if you're doing, if you're changing classes, what classes you'd be in and what you know and what you don't, so they know what to teach you by marking and that.*

[A test] indicates to the teacher sort of what group you'd be in; what level group you'd be in for learning and [to] see what, sort of, you need to learn more, and stuff.

Either way, learners maintain they do not know they have learnt until they receive a quantifiable indication that they have. Their reliance on the teacher during this initial phase of self-assessment is evident because, as one student put it, "If you don't have a test, you don't know what you know."

Students view tests as having two key functions. First, tests help group students for subjects such as mathematics. Second, they identify for the teacher what students need to learn. Most students in this study were familiar with the pre- and post-testing in mathematics that were an integral part of their school's programme. However, although they noted they had learnt when going from a low pretest score to a high post-test score, they could only identify that they had learnt—not what they had learnt, or what they still needed to learn:

S: *Yes, we have maths tests, we have all sorts of tests.*
R: *Okay, can you tell me about the maths tests?*
S: *Um, well, they go into home sample, [portfolios] and you get a piece of paper, and it has all these questions on it, and it gets put in a file or something from you, and it's got all the answers and what your maths age is and stuff like that.*
R: *Your maths age?*
S: *Yeah, like, um, I'm in special needs for maths so I could be, like, a seven-year-old maths age or eight or nine. [The student was 12 years old.]*
R: *Well, if you have the tests to start with, then why do you have that test to find out where you're going to be? Why do you have that test?*
S: *To find out what you need to learn, to find out what age so they can teach you that age and just know where you are.*
R: *Okay, and then you have some lessons, and then do you have another test after that?*
S: *Yeah.*
R: *Well, what's that one?*
S: *That one is to see if you've made your age higher, so you're up to another age or you're at the same, and you need to be re-taught it or, um, to see if you've forgotten it—see if you've gone down or up in your marks.*
R: *If you go up in your marks, what does that mean?*

S: Well, then you get taught harder stuff.
R: Okay. What does it tell you about your learning if you go up in your marks?
S: Then that means that I've learnt something.
R: And what if you go down in your marks?
S: I'm losing my memory. I'm badder than I was.
R: Is that possible?
S: It is possible.
R: Do you usually go up or down?
S: At my other school I was going up and at this school I've only had one test, so I'm not quite sure yet.

The last statement, "I'm not quite sure yet", indicates the student's lack of awareness about his learning and an inability to self-assess his learning without support or guidance. Although this student had been at the school for nearly six months, he maintained a lack of awareness of his learning until his mark from the test came through. He did not know or could not guess whether he had learnt enough in a mathematics unit to increase his score. Although he had completed the test, and was therefore aware of its content, he still relied on the test score to help him self-assess his learning.

The participating students were affected by poor grades, either because they were teased or because of the associated competition within their peer group. Some students used grades as a means of denoting status and rank in the classroom. Public exposure of the grades was therefore a source of embarrassment or delight. Said one student:

> ... people tease you, and it, sometimes it's really hard to learn if you know you're going to get really low; it's easier to do, um, the stuff you've learnt than new stuff.

Said another:

> Some people put you down, and I feel really sad, but when you come up and do really good and be better than they are, then it puts you on a higher scale than they are, because they put you down, they think you're not that good, but when you beat them, it feels so great you just proved them wrong.

The students' tendency to use test scores to measure their achievement in relation to that of peers became competitive at times: students—predominantly male—commented about feeling "choice" when they beat other students, although some expressed this in terms of bettering themselves and using the grades as the vehicle to identify whether they had learnt. Often, beating their peers conferred a sense of bettering themselves:

You don't try and beat others, you're just trying to better yourself ... You're also wanting to be as good as a mate ... you want to be as good as other people as well, and also better yourself, to reach your standard, as well.

It will make you look better; everyone will see you as better than them, and they'll start being friends with you, and all that.

Students used grades first to indicate learning had occurred and second to gain membership of a group, such as a higher mathematics group. For the student in the following extract, membership of the higher mathematics group equated with further learning because he would be introduced to "harder stuff":

It's, like, me and my friends, like, we go, ha ha, I got higher than you ... because if we're in the higher group, we'll learn more stuff and harder stuff.

When marks became important to the students, they used several strategies to increase their own mark and/or to prevent others from attaining the same level. While students referred to helping one another, and provided illustrations of this, some kept certain skills and strategies to themselves if they thought teaching it to their peers would advantage them grade wise. One boy, for example, said that he did not want other students in his technicraft class in on his secret for producing particularly good rounded corners on pencil cases (which the class were making at the time) because "I don't want them to get a better one [mark] than me, or a better pencil case than me or ... because I want to get an A or B or whatever, but I don't want to get a useless mark." This student was able to self-assess his work, but he still wanted the teacher to confirm it by way of a more than "useless mark".

In learning situations out of school, external evaluations helped students identify the level of their performance. For example, one student said his judo assessments identified progress because these determined if he would go up from one grade to the next and thereby gain an advanced colour belt. In another example, a student who performed regularly in speech competitions and examinations said he could tell how well he was performing by the facial appearance of the judge. However, he went on to explain that he did not rely solely on this form of feedback; he also needed a grade. His concern lay not just in identifying he had learnt (Category A), but in wanting to know how *well* he had learnt (Category B):

> S: When you're doing speech competition, if the judge is looking pretty grrrr, you know you've got a bit of a problem, but you can't really tell, but if she's smiling at you, you normally get first place. But if she looks angry, but you don't really think that because you're enjoying yourself, you get second or third, so it doesn't really matter.
> R: That's interesting.
> S: That's what I found out this time. But that also sort of happens in exams as well.
> R: Okay, so you get some feedback by how the other person is looking, how the examiner is looking before you get the results?
> S: Yeah. I have to be happy with myself first.
> R: How do you know you're happy with yourself? What do you need to have done?
> S: Oh, you have to have tried your best and you've got to be positive that you've done all to your ability, and so then if you think you've really done well, it doesn't matter if you don't get top or not. But even if you don't get that, well there's always next time.

Performing (C): What did I learn?

Reliance on an external source such as a teacher, parent or peer (Category A) and a grade or outcome from a test or competition (Category B) are the key sources of information that learners in these categories use to determine whether and what they have learnt. While some learners do not go beyond these stages, others begin to show an awareness of learning through their *performance* of an activity or task. As one participating student stated:

> I know that I know my times tables because I can say them, and I know them because I can say them correctly and fluently now.

This third conceptualisation is a more sophisticated one than the earlier conceptualisations because learners are beginning to develop an inclination to reflect when assessing their performance either during or after the task. They are beginning to appreciate that they need to listen to and watch others and then reflect on that information in regard to their own performance on a task or activity:

> *You've got to listen to people and then know what they do and how they do it, and then that's how you better yourself.*

This stage is categorised by the sense of *doing* and of achievement. One student said he knew he had learnt when he felt fulfilled:

> *I actually know I've learnt it ... like, I don't know why, I just know I've learnt it. I think it's the way I feel. It's just like that bit's fulfilled in my head—it's just a feeling.*

This boy had earlier said that he enjoyed working on activities he knew he could successfully achieve:

> *I really like doing the stuff that I'm good at because I know that I'm good enough to actually have a good go at it.*

Another student said that he knew when his performance was "alright", and that, for him, the self-assessment process was one accomplished" in my head":

> *When I'm at home, I sort of, just, sort of think it's alright. I sort of do it in my head. If you think you've done your hardest and you're really pleased with yourself, you can feel choice.*

When talking about an activity they had performed or a task they had completed, the students who held a conception of self-assessment in this Category C typically said that feeling confident about their performance contributed to a sense of knowing or awareness of learning. "If," said one student, "you're not confident, you're not going to get anywhere, because you've got to know that you can do it." Said another, "... you just know for yourself—self-confidence or something, I don't know." A third had this to say:

> *You actually recognise yourself as having been able to do it, and then the teacher would see your work, and then she'd know. You know what you're doing, and something clicks in your mind, and you suddenly know it, and after a little bit of practice, it will be good.*

Despite this growing sense of awareness, the students' comments revealed that when, in a classroom setting, their teacher asked them to record their self-assessments for him or her, the students recorded a grade or mark that met their peers' expectations (peer pressure) that they remain humble but still not put themselves down, as the following student put it:

You usually put your own work down so you don't show off. If there's a 'good', an 'excellent', a 'not so good' and a 'poor' one, you put it about half way, and then you don't, you're not putting yourself down, and you're not saying you're really good either, so long as you do that.

Students who held Category C conceptions of self-assessment demonstrated that self-assessment is more than just acquiring confirmation of learning through seeking others' opinions or through a grade, as is evident in the next extract. The student who features said he knew how well he was doing when playing competitive tennis not only because, "Well, you win … but you also see improvement." He further explained:

Like, if you're not a very good server, and you might not win the game, but you get a couple of ace serves, and so you know that you've got better.

The same student found he needed some kind of performance to enhance his understanding of a story; for example, to understand a novel, he needed to watch a movie. Consequently, his self-assessment was based on and linked to his knowledge of how he learnt best:

You can't read a book and know all the meaning about it. You'd have to see it in a movie to understand.

Students need to have opportunities to perform tasks that allow them to use the knowledge they have acquired. This is illustrated in the following extract. Here, the student explains her need to use her acquired skills in order to know she has learnt. Sometimes, she says, she does not know she has learnt until she uses these skills, often long after the learning took place:

S: I think you only learn it, you only know when you've learnt it, is when you actually use it. Like, I was watching Animal Hospital [a television programme] and so maybe when I get older some of those things will help me, but I actually don't know that I've learnt them. Like, I was listening to some of the words and some of the things they called the animals,

> so I actually never know that I've actually used it until I write a ... I might write a speech about it, or we might do a topic on it. So I never really know until I've actually used it.
>
> R: Do you have to use everything you learn?
>
> S: No, no, some of it's just, just something that you just take in, and it's always there. I'm not, I'm not really, sometimes I might learn about, um ... it might be about, oh ... I might learn about some kind of sport game, although I do like it, but sometimes I don't actually remember that I've actually learnt it until I actually play the game. And sometimes, like, my mum and dad might tell me about, um, how to avoid getting stressed out, and if you're, if you're like, um ... how to use it and whenever, I always do that. Like [when] I play cricket, I always remember what my dad would say, about making sure that the ball links up to your shoulder, and so I'd always remember that, and so when you use it, when you get older or when you're doing it in sports or something, that's when you remember that you've actually learnt it.

Towards the end of the interview, she reiterated her main point: "… you don't really, really know until you've actually used the knowledge that you've learnt".

Students with a conception of self-assessment within this category not only used their performance to self-assess their learning but also tended to draw on their learning to provide a solution to some activity that did not work the first time. As one boy explained, "You have to do another way of doing it ... look at a different way of finding the answer." He continued:

> Yes, because if you look at something in maths at a particular problem solving thing, it might not work out, so you have to do another way of doing it, so you sort of have to, um, look at a different way of finding the answer. You just check it, guess, and check that one, [then] just get other ones. Well, you try something, and you might not be good at it, then you learn something new to make it better, and then you do it again, using the thing that you've learnt, something you've learnt—and then you're better at it.

In this next example of performance being used to self-assess learning, the student explains why she knew her earlier performance naming musical notes from manuscript required her to engage in further learning:

> R: When you said you had to figure out another way of doing it because you weren't very good, how did you know you weren't very good?

S: Well, it wasn't a quick reaction. I was saying now that's ... C, so I'd have to count up the note from the note that I already knew, so I wasn't very, yeah, I'd have to count up, but now I can say, yeah, that's C.

Through their increased emphasis on their own self-assessment of their performances and as they become increasingly aware of their role in the learning process, learners take more control of the self-assessment process. In contrast to Category A, learners who hold a more sophisticated conception of self-assessment (Category C), employ other sources—such as books, flash cards, computers—in a more independent and intentional manner to self-assess their learning. One interesting example was related by a student who had completed a science experiment using lemons to build a circuit. She used instructions from a book, which said lemons could indeed be used, and her teacher confirmed it should work:

R: So can you tell me something that you've done this year that you didn't know before?
S: How to make a science project.
R: Can you tell me about that?
S: Um, well, we had to do a aim and what we did for our experiment, and do the experiment, and do up the results and stuff on any subject, and you got to pick and do all these weird things.
R: What sort of weird things?
S: Um, like, draw a conclusion, and everything had to match the other things, and all the answers from our experiment, if it didn't work and if it worked, then what we did and stuff.
R: What was your topic?
S: Silicon circuit.
R: Okay, what did you learn about the silicon circuit?
S: That if you, like, see an experiment in a book or something, it doesn't always work, because I tried to make a light with a battery using a lemon as a power source, and it didn't work, so that it will light, and you've got lots of different bulbs and different size lemons, and it still didn't work.
R: Why?
S: I don't know.
R: Should it have worked?

    S: Yeah.
    R: How do you know it should have worked?
    S: Because the book said it would.

This student's use of the science book shows she was not relying on the teacher or the grade to assess her learning. Rather, she was doing this in relation to the information in the book. When her experiment did not work, she was not sure if she had actually learnt that lemons can complete a circuit: the book said it could, but she hadn't seen any evidence to confirm it. The student's activity throughout the process, including her interpretation of the information from the science book, her involvement in the science experiment and her self-assessment of what should have happened and what, in fact, did happen, highlights the interaction between self-assessment and learning.

Another student explained her use of flash cards to learn music notes. These were a series of cards with musical notes written on manuscript on one side and the corresponding letter name on the other. For example, if C sharp was written on the manuscript on one side of the card, the student would state what the note was and then turn over the card that had the letter name written on it. In this way, the student could confirm whether the note she had identified was correct.

Category C in relation to out-of-school learning activities such as music, dancing, speech, judo, mountain-bike riding or other sports is characterised by the ability to perform. In the following extract, a student became aware of her dodging ability in netball through her performance. She did not rely on her coach's feedback to know she had learnt how to dodge. Using the information from her performance allowed her to identify the skill she had learnt:

    S: *I enjoy dodging because I think I'm good at that.*
    R: *How do you know you're good at dodging?*
    S: *Because I can see that if I'm dodging one person and I can get the ball easily. I did it when I was in Rangitāne. I played, and there was boys, and I played with them, and I knew that I was good. I think I was the great player then because I knew I dodged the ball really good.*
    R: *Did you know you dodged the ball really well because the teacher told you or because you just knew it?*

> S: *I knew it. Yes, I knew it ... and the teacher told me when I went to ask her what things I should be good at.*

This student, along with other Category C students, also mentioned using peers' performance as a point of reference for her own understanding of her learning. She said that in a game of netball, "If I do something wrong, I just copy someone." This use of peers as a reference point to gauge learning differs from the Category B approach, where grades denote competitive edge. Learners who conceptualised self-assessment within Category C use peers in a substantially different and more enlightening way. By identifying how their performance compares with that of their peers, they can *enhance* their own performance. Whenever, throughout the interviews, the students described using peers in this way, they conveyed a sense of being aware of their learning. In this next extract, the student describes using her peers to determine the accuracy of her dance performance. She told me she needed to have her head in the correct position but that sometimes her head did not look "the right way":

> R: *How do you know if your head is not looking the right way?*
> S: *Sometimes other kids in the group are doing it one way, and you think you might be doing it the other, yeah. Sometimes the teacher will just go, 'Oh, your head is looking the wrong way,' or something.*
> R: *Okay, so it's either looking at the other kids and seeing what they're doing or ...*
> S: *Yeah, we've only got a really small group this year, but last year there was, oh well, there was a few, you know about six or seven, and we used to do it on our own, you know, to check how the other person was doing it, and so the teacher could pay attention to that child, and then we could all see the way they're doing it and if we're doing it slightly different to them. And if the teacher says they're doing it right, then you've got to try and do it the same as them, or you know if you're doing it slightly different.*

Using criteria (D): Do I understand what I have learnt?

The fourth category of learner self-assessment is identified by the way learners see their role in the assessment process. Learners who hold conceptions of self-assessment within this category are increasingly reflective about their performance and view themselves as integral to the learning and assessment process. Rather than relying on other sources, such as parents and teachers (Category A), grades (Category B) or even their own performance (Category C), these learners go a step further by using identified criteria, such as teacher benchmarks, to assess their performance. This category is more sophisticated than the earlier categories because learners take more control and responsibility for the self-assessment process.

The following extracts from interviews with two students who conceptualise self-assessment as using criteria (Category D) illustrate the tendency to use adults as models to provide the criteria or benchmark against which to measure their own performance. The learning activity is playing the piano:

> *When it sounds like it's right, because you sort of have an ear to music I find. And, like, if it sounds right, because my parents, usually she always plays the whole thing first, and then I just try and do it myself and listen for it. You know because you can tell when it's supposed to be B flat and that's because it's supposed to sound low instead of normal or high instead of normal.*

> *Well, I would've heard the piece because my teacher would've played it to me and I would know, I would remember how it went, and then I'd see if my playing was the same. If I've hit the wrong note, then it doesn't sound right, and ... well, my teacher said I've got a good memory for music, so once I know, like, a bar, I could hear that bar and almost play it. I know if it's wrong because I can remember what it's meant to be like.*

One of the critical features of this category is that learners express an awareness of the criteria associated with the learning task. They are increasingly aware of *what* they are learning and *how* they are learning it, whereas the learners in the previous categories are more concerned with these questions: "Have I learnt?" "How much have I learnt?" "What did I learn?"

The use of criteria enables learners to recognise the difference between being able to do something or not do something, as well as to identify their areas of achievement or difficulty. These learners demonstrate a growing interest in knowing exactly what they have achieved in terms of learning outcomes, and they show a developing independence from the teacher.

When learners become more aware of their learning and are able to place less reliance and emphasis on the teacher's evaluation or other forms of external evaluation of their learning, they assume a greater role in the self-assessment process. After completing an activity, they are able to show more awareness that they have learnt something; more importantly, they can also identify this "something". As in Category C, the learners are beginning to show confidence in their ability to self-assess their learning.

In learning situations that were product or performance oriented, the students in my study who held Category D conceptions of self-assessment often relied at least as much on their own evaluations as on evaluations by others. One student noted that even if his teacher gave him a good evaluation on something he had made, it would not influence his own self-assessment if he himself did not feel it was a good piece of work, "… if you don't like what you've made, you don't use it much when you get it home. You throw it in the rubbish when you get home."

For learners, ability to identify the teacher's established criteria is part of knowing what aspects make up the learning task. It also helps them self-assess in relation to the explicit, teacher-led criteria. Learners have a rationale for what they are doing and a sense of purpose beyond getting something "right". Learners who hold conceptions of self-assessment within Category D believe they can improve, and they show an increased awareness of *how* to improve. Students who hold less sophisticated conceptions of self-assesment believe the only way to improve is through practice, because speed and accuracy are determining features of learning. In contrast, students who hold a more sophisticated conception (Category D) are aware they can learn from their mistakes as well as from teaching their peers. For them the emphasis on being correct all the time has diminished.

Category D is thus characterised by learners who are becoming increasingly confident in their ability to understand the nature of the task, to identify the criteria for measuring the learning outcome and to teach their peers as a function of their own self-assessment. Teaching or supporting peers through the learning process is an aspect of self-assessment because the students need first to identify the criteria to assess their own learning and, second, to use those criteria and their self-assessment of their performance to teach others. For these students, use of peers to self-assess was not organised by the teacher and the students were not requested to teach their peers; they did so as a natural part of the self-assessment process. As one student explained, "If I've finished mine, I usually help him in his, and it gets him actually moving."

Learners help their peers when they have mastered a concept. Because they feel confident in their own ability to perform the task and because they understand the reasoning behind the concept, they are able to talk it through with friends who are struggling. The following extracts from two different students illustrate this process:

> S: *My friend didn't really understand how to rename numbers so I, we kind of were talking this morning, and she got it, so she understands it now.*
>
> R: *Does she understand it now?*
>
> S: *Well, she sort of knew, but she was having trouble. You talk to her and show her again, and she tries it once more, and she gets it wrong, and so you go over it again. And she looks at yours, and then she looks at her own, and then she works out what's wrong, and then you write it down. Sometimes it's easier for kids because the teacher goes on about a whole lot that you don't really want to know, but they don't really understand what you're having trouble with sometimes, and the kids do because they have trouble with the same thing.*

> S: *Mary, she was sitting next to me, she's one of my friends, she didn't understand it [a mathematics concept], so I explained it to her, and we got going.*
>
> R: *Okay, when you explained it to Mary, how did you know when she finally got it?*
>
> S: *Because she sort of explained it back to me, what to do, and she measured one, and said, 'Oh, T goes there,' and stuff.*

Implicit in these two examples is the notion that learners are most likely to view teaching their peers as an indicator of their *own* learning.

When referring to community-learning contexts, the students similarly reported teaching their friends once they knew, from assessing their own learning, that they understood the task. As this student explains, with regard to netball, students often experience the same difficulties themselves before mastering and understanding the concept, and it is this knowledge of the struggle that often helps them help their peers:

> *You're learning how to do them properly and what you were doing wrong to show somebody else, because if they're doing the same thing as you were doing, you can say, 'Well, this is what you were doing wrong, because it happened to me.'*

Setting learning goals (E): What do I want to learn?

Despite having a relatively sophisticated awareness of learning within Category D, learners do not see an internal relationship between themselves as learners and the world they experience. They view learning and assessment as separate. In contrast, learners who conceptualise self-assessment within Category E are characterised by their more sophisticated way of experiencing the world. They demonstrate an awareness of their own understanding and knowledge—their learning—in relation to their self-assessments. Category E is more sophisticated than the previous categories because learners first establish the criteria for assessment, then use these criteria to assess their learning. In contrast, learners who conceptualise self-assessment within Category D use benchmarks set by the teachers or their peers as their criteria for assessing their performance. A learner who conceptualises self-assessment as setting learning goals (Category E) is also characterised by the realisation that there is often no longer "one right answer" to a problem but, rather, multiple perspectives.

As learners became more confident that they understand the concept they are learning, their interest grows and they are able to identify various perspectives and possibilities. They develop their own criteria for self-assessment, set personal goals and believe in their own ability. Sometimes, they do not share these goals with others, including their teachers, as this example illustrates:

> *I just wouldn't tell anyone, you know, my goals or anything. I'd just do them myself, and then I'd just think of my performance, what I think, how well I think I have done, but, you know, I wouldn't mention it to anyone else. If I didn't have any goals, I wouldn't really know what to go for to try to achieve. You'd always have to have a goal.*

Learners who view self-assessment according to the conceptions that characterise this category are more aware of their capabilities than are learners with less sophisticated conceptions. Because these learners have learning aims that often differ from those of their teachers, their solutions to a problem or learning outcome can differ from the teachers'. A student in a class that designed and made tepees provides an interesting example. He acknowledged his capability to complete a teacher-assigned task to design and construct a tepee, but he also knew he had not completed it as the teacher intended, nor according to the specified criteria; he therefore received a lower grade—a grade that did not represent his knowledge. Nevertheless, he did not consider the grade reflected what he could do. Instead, he placed higher priority on his knowledge of his ability. The relationship between motivation and ability to perform is highlighted well in this example, and provides a poignant reminder that "there is an important distinction between what children can do and what children will do on any given occasion" (Broadfoot et al., 1991, p. 166):

> S: Another boy in our class, we're making tepees, and he made this real choice one, that had bow and arrow, and it was perfect, and he got a twenty or something out of twenty, and he felt real good because he beat everyone else. Because we only, well, I haven't been graded yet, but no one else got twenty out of twenty.
> R: Do you think he was pleased because of the high mark or because he liked his tepee?
> S: Because, well, he beat other people, and he's successful and he's happy with his tepee.
> R: So your tepee hasn't been evaluated yet?
> S: No.
> R: What do you reckon that will get?
> S: Well, my one, it's only out of ten, because, um, mine's out of ten because if we bring it on Monday, it will be out of twenty, but if you brung it today it would be out of ten.
> R: Okay.
> S: And I think I'll get about a five because it's too bright and it doesn't have the sticks out the top.
> R: So why didn't you put the sticks out the top?
> S: Because I didn't have enough time.
> R: And why is it too bright?
> S: Because I couldn't get any dark paints that go on material.

During the interview, this student explained that he knew the set of criteria used for grading. If he had adhered to the identified criteria, he would have exemplified an earlier conception of self-assessment (Category D). However, for his own self-assessment, he went beyond the teacher's identified criteria for the project by adopting a learning outcome governed by his personal goal. He could explain the teacher-specified components for the tepee design and construction, and he was aware that the mark he received for his construction would be based on these. Nevertheless, he seemed not to share his teacher's learning goals in relation to the activity or perhaps did not understand the point behind his teacher's goals. Clearly, making a tepee was not *his* goal, because, as he said, "You're not going to exactly live in a tepee when you grow older, so you don't really need to know that."

This boy and the other students who held this conceptualisation of self-assessment (Category E) demonstrated an awareness that grades do not necessarily represent their knowing. They were also aware they could improve their performance. The next two examples show students no longer needing the teacher or the grade to verify their understanding of the concept because they have *self-knowledge* of their capabilities in relation to the task. In the first example, the student began by telling me that she set herself goals then evaluated them independently from the teacher or from checklists provided by the teacher. She then said:

Before I do something I often set myself a small goal and then if I fulfil that goal, I self-evaluate. I often don't tell someone about my goal. I think to myself I'll do this, and if I do it, then I'd say well done.

The second student alluded to the power of motivation when she said:

If I actually really, really, really want to do it, then I set that goal and, like, I usually get, I usually am able to do that by the date that I set.

For these two students, self-assessment of their work was part of, not separate from, their learning. They viewed self-assessment as part of the learning process because it is part of setting learning goals, as the first student pointed out.

I found that the students who set goals and were happy with their subsequent performance were clearly satisfied with their learning. They could see the relevance of self-assessment, particularly when they felt they had learnt something. One student told me that his assessment of his poem, especially the words he used in it, were integral to his belief he had written a good poem. He evaluated it as good on the basis of his own, rather than his teacher's, evaluation. When I asked him how he knew the poem was good, he replied:

> S: I know [it's good] because of the words that I've used and, like, we did an upside-down poem. Like, we wrote the real poem about camp and then upside down, and the teacher liked it because I had used a word—'slithery'. I had just learnt that the same day. Somebody else used it, so I, like, checked up in the dictionary, and it like means fast and really slippery, so I, like, thought it was a good word to, like, use—very slithery and fast.
>
> R: So do you know that something is good because you like it or because the teacher tells you it's good?
>
> S: Because I like the word, like what it means when I describe something.

Another student also told me of the satisfaction he gained from learning that was part of the self-assessment process. He indicated that being happy with what he had achieved was the important factor, and that even if the score he obtained for his work was not "the greatest in the world", he could improve next time:

> *Well, if you're happy with your score, well, if you're happy with what you've done before knowing your score, well, then you, um ... just seem to ... you don't need to have the greatest score in the world, but you know that you can, at least next time you do it, you'll be able to do it better; you won't be all tensed up inside.*

Sometimes, learners can identify what they need to learn or perform but barriers to learning prevent them (usually temporarily) from achieving their goals. This is illustrated in a transcript from an observation during a Saturday morning trampolining class, in which the student was attempting a difficult manoeuvre on a trampoline:

> *Susan has her run and she completes a sit ... turn sit ... back turn up ... backward flip ... tuck ... layout back ... (pike back) forward flip. She did this too fast and landed on her knees. Susan came over to me after she had finished. She explained what she was trying to do and that she had been trying this particular manoeuvre for a few months. She could explain what she needed to do, and could execute the entire movement, but could not land on her feet. She always landed on her knees and fell forward. I asked her how she learnt to do a backward flip. She explained it was easy because two people held her while she went over so she could get an idea of the movement. She prefers the back tuck because 'It's not so scary.' However, when she performs the pike back, where her legs are straight, she sometimes feels she is not in control. Susan has moved through a series of badges. She ran and got the badges to explain*

what she was doing. She had completed in this order ... Red ... Blue ... Green ... Yellow, and was now working on the Black badge. The move that is holding her back is a Crash Dive Bail Out. She can explain what she has to do and can do parts of it in isolation, but cannot execute the entire movement.

Evaluating learning content (F): Is this worth learning?

Limited evidence suggested some students held a further conception of self-assessment that formed a sixth category (F). This, the most sophisticated and inclusive category, is distinguished from previous categories by the fact that learners assess the *value* of the learning content in relation to their own needs. While this process occurs to some degree in the earlier categories, Category F is characterised by learners who consider the relationship between the nominal learning objective and their personal learning objectives. They go beyond merely wondering why they are learning or why they want to be bothered learning; they consciously decide the learning has inherent value rather than simply deciding they do or do not want to learn.

The student quoted below told me she learnt something new every day. She made choices about what learning was of value and, having done so, passed on this knowledge to her friends:

> *I learn a new thing every day. Like, sometimes they have facts on the radio and I think, 'Oh, that's good,' and then I come to school and tell all my friends, and then they tell me something.*

Category F is also characterised by learners' awareness of themselves in relation to the worth of learning. It goes beyond the question, often asked by children of school age, "Why do I need to learn this?" The worth of learning is about the relationship students develop between the knowledge they want to gain and the knowledge they already have. This worth is closely connected to personal goals and motivation for learning. The boy who described the design and production of a tepee provides an example of this notion. When I asked him about the criteria for designing the tepee, he explained:

> S: *We were given a sheet that said what you'd get higher points with, like, we'd get one for if it [the tepee] was steady and it wouldn't blow over. And there's this girl, and if you just*

touched it, it would fall over, and she got marked down for that. And my one, well, it says it has to have a hole up top—my one's got a hole, but it doesn't have the sticks to hold the hole open. And it said background, for, like, tepee bows, arrows, tomahawks, things that stretch the buffalo skin, and stuff like that.

R: So did you follow through that?

S: I tried to, but my colours, I tried to go the closest colours and materials but something that would probably feel like buffalo skin. And some of them used leather, some of them used material, someone used wrapping paper, some just used cardboard, and made their whole tepee out of cardboard.

R: So what was your one made out of?

S: Material and paper. Paper on the inside and material over it.

I then asked him if he was concerned about what he was graded on. He said that it did worry him "for some stuff", but not for the tepee. His next words, which I quoted earlier in this chapter, are worth repeating because they so clearly exemplify the tendency of Category F learners to evaluate their learning against knowledge they perceive has worth:

Well you don't really need to know how if you're going to make a tepee when you grow up because there's houses—you're not going to exactly live in a tepee when you grow older, so you don't really need to know that, so you don't really care about that. But for stuff like woodwork and metalwork and that sort of stuff, that you really need to know.

Learners who use their own criteria when self-assessing generally identify the need to be honest with their self-assessment. The following student believed that even if he gave himself a better grade or inflated his belief about the quality of his work, it wouldn't actually make the work better. "If I got it wrong," he said, "I just have to face it and be honest … because I'm not with my evaluations, I'm not really cheating anyone but myself if I did." He later added that if he wrote the self-assessment "better, that won't make it [the work] better".

When evaluating learning content or a task, the students who conceptualised self-assessment as evaluating content (Category F) were those most likely across the categories to persevere with challenging learning situations. One student explained he needed to look at different ways of solving the problem if he could not solve it on the first attempt. As one student said, "You have to do another way of doing it ... [you have] to look at a different way of finding the answer." But these students generally also self-assessed their learning in this situation by asking themselves if the required learning was worthy of their perseverance.

Self-assessment: The dilemma for teachers

Understanding students' conceptions of self-assessment is important for teaching because it enhances both teachers' and students' learning about learning. Students who self-assess in increasingly sophisticated ways are more likely to be motivated to pursue learning goals. The outcomes of that learning are evident. Learners who do not rely purely on marks and grades to know they have learnt are better positioned to challenge their own thinking in realms beyond their immediate world. In contrast, when students remain dependent on an outside source (grades, marks, teacher) to confirm their learning, they are less likely to actively set learning goals, use criteria for assessment or develop their own criteria to assess their learning. Such students are unlikely to become independent, intentional learners unless their view of learning and self-assessment is challenged and changed. This consideration presents a particular challenge for teachers because if students continue to view learning as that which can be measured and defined quantitatively, they will continue to approach learning tasks in a superficial manner.

Although educators have long held the belief that radical changes to assessment systems in schools will bring about a general reform of educational practices, this approach will not address the way students experience assessment through pedagogy and curriculum; a change in the way we view and value learning and self-assessment will. Furthermore, the *technique* behind assessment practices will not make a difference to students' conceptions of learning and self-assessment if it is still couched in the institutional mould. So, although we might generally agree that "pupil assessment is crucial in bringing about reform" (Holloway, 2000, p. 84), it is the *role* students play in this process that will make the difference. *The New Zealand Curriculum* (Ministry of Education, 2007) places the learner at the centre of this process; how this position is to be accomplished is less defined. The intent is that "when teachers and students join together in defining what is worth knowing—the key task in creating the curriculum—they engage in meaningful work that reflects the content and concepts they both value" (Raider-Roth, 2005, p. 159).

The New Zealand Curriculum is also the main guide on assessment for New Zealand teachers. The curriculum document provides a clear directive to schools—"to improve students' learning and teachers' teaching as both student and teacher respond to the information that it provides" (Ministry of Education, 2007, p. 39). However, teachers often experience the tension that arises when they use qualitative self-assessment practices to improve student learning but feel compelled to use quantitative assessment practices that the Ministry of Education and ERO require (Bourke & Willis, 1998; Thrupp & Smith, 1999). In the late 1990s, Thrupp and Smith (1999) argued, "teachers appear to have begun to internalise a new set of values and practices related to ERO's review requirements" (p. 195). Several years later, Crooks (2006) claimed this was still the case: "school personnel often perceive ERO to have too high an emphasis on school policies and paperwork, and too little emphasis on the realities of classroom programmes and student engagement" (p. 15).

In the classroom context, the teacher-initiated self-assessment practices identified in this study would be better described as *institutionalised* self-assessment because teachers, while attempting to introduce authentic assessment measures, do so within the constraints of the institutional context of the school, Ministry of Education assessment policy and ERO requirements. One reason for this is that despite the argument that one of the functions of assessment is to facilitate better learning (Black, 1993; Gipps, 1994), teachers still tend to use assessment as a tool for accountability rather than learning (Black, 1993; Bourke & Willis, 1998). In England and Wales, the introduction of Standard Assessment Tasks (SAT) for seven-year-olds (1990) and 14-year-olds (1992) negatively affected teaching practice, teachers' morale and student motivation (Pollard et al., 1994). Some teachers became "assessment magpies, collecting and storing performance evidence and information at every possible opportunity but making little use of it to adjust the learning program of individual pupils" (Black, 1994, p. 197). In the United States, a similar assessment situation occurred as a reaction to a model of "data-driven decision making" (Nichols & Singer, 2000, p. 34; Noyce, Perda, & Traver, 2000). As discussed in Chapter 5, the introduction of the Education (National Standards) Amendment Act 2008 in New Zealand will further influence how teachers and students conceptualise learning and self-assessment. Wiliam (2010) reviewed the research evidence on the effects of assessment and high-stakes accountability tests on student achievement and concluded that while there were unintended outcomes, a standards-based approach did raise student achievement, "It has been widely observed for many years that when any test (or indeed any other performance indicator) is made the focus of public policy attention, then performance as measured by that test improves" (p. 116). However, he cautioned that the research also showed that, in the context of such a regime, teachers are influenced to adjust their teaching to the test and its prescribed outcomes.

In essence, what the students in this study tell us is that when self-assessment is introduced and identified as "assessment" in the classroom, it diminishes the value of self-assessment as an integral part of learning. However, learners who initiate personal (and often private) self-assessment, learning goals and criteria for evaluating these goals, tend to make little distinction between the learning and assessment aspects of self-assessment. Teachers can encourage the association between learning and self-assessment by talking to students about *accessing* their knowledge rather than *assessing* outcomes. This occurs best when students are encouraged to talk about their learning within the multiple settings in which they live and learn.

Summary

All students in this study used external sources of feedback to assess their own learning. They accessed information about their work either from others (peers, parents and teachers) or from artefacts (stars, stamps, stickers and grades). The common elements that characterised these sources as vehicles for assessment were why and how the students used the information these provided. For some students (those with the least sophisticated conceptions of self-assessment), these sources were the only ways they had to know they had learnt. For others (those who held the more sophisticated conceptions), these sources still provided evidence but evidence that they interpreted in different ways or did not agree with. All students were thus aware of having learnt something, and so held a conception of self-assessment.

A good starting point for all teachers intent on facilitating students' self-assessment is to recognise that students employ a range of means to "self-assess". Increasingly sophisticated forms of self-assessment can be developed despite the constraints of externally mandated assessment approaches often present for both teacher and learner. A sophisticated conception of self-assessment relies on both teacher and learner *valuing* learning, not just outcomes or grades. This type of understanding of and use of self-assessment is the one most likely to prepare learners for the multiplicity of learning contexts and personal and vocational changes that they will experience throughout their lives. The next, and final, chapter picks up on this notion.

CHAPTER 7

The learner and context: Enjoying the edge of incompetence

> It is now Deb's turn to abseil down the cliff. She has on all the equipment, ropes and safety harness. She is at the top of the cliff receiving instructions from the instructor. She was told by the instructor to put her hair (which is in a long ponytail) down her T shirt. Deb seems terrified. The instructor said to her, 'Just remember that nothing can happen to you.' Deb started, then said, 'I can't do that.' She got her foot on one ledge and was told by the instructor to position her other foot. Again she said, 'I can't do that.' When she got down the cliff, she was more relaxed and seemed pleased to have conquered it. I ask her how she found it and she said, with a broad smile, 'It was bloody scary.' (Bourke, 2000, p. 205)

The day Deb learnt to abseil, she conquered a fear and became part of a community of learners who can say, "I have abseiled. I know how it feels." She did not say, "I am an abseiler", and she would not be likely to do so until she was at a stage where she could identify this activity with who she is. While not all learning is scary, or necessarily exciting or thrilling for the learner, the process of knowing *about* something to *experiencing* it—of experiencing the unknown and ultimately understanding it—involves the type of learning that influences and informs who we are, so forging an inextricable link with identity. Deb did not start out as an abseiler, nor did she finish as one, but she did get a sense of what that might mean. She moved from being scared to being thrilled. Her instructor was supportive and instilled in Deb the belief that she could—and would—learn to abseil that day. This example illustrates how learners can be challenged in a supportive learning environment. While the context is abseiling, the principle applies equally to the classroom. *The New Zealand Curriculum* promotes the idea that learners "should experience a curriculum that engages and challenges them" (Ministry of Education, 2007, p. 9); in effect suggesting, metaphorically at least, that learners should abseil every day.

Accepting a "risk environment" for learning is healthy. The sense of challenge and the scary feeling that come with learning need to be recognised as important and legitimate. As Rogoff (1990) puts it, "learning involves functioning at the edge of one's competence on the border of incompetence" (p. 202). Learners are adventurers; they must be prepared to risk failing—or failing with support—on the way to learning a new skill. Learners operate in more than one context, and they often change roles accordingly (Boaler, 1993). Rogoff and Toma (1997) point out that "flexibility is likely to be useful or even necessary in the complexity of everyday life in today's world" (p. 492). Different contexts provide different opportunities and varying comfort zones in which to explore learning. In order to learn, learners adapt to these contexts and allow themselves to be challenged in different roles; feeling less confident in some but secure in others. Active learning is evident in young people when they understand what they are doing and why, when they have fun and are challenged. In these cases, teachers seldom need to question whether a learner is "engaged".

Focusing on the role learners take in a learning setting and recognising how roles and conceptions of learning change across multiple settings allows new pictures about learning to emerge. In this chapter, I consider how learners identify and adopt different roles for their learning, according to context. These include the goal setter, the self-assessor, the peer teacher, the peer assessor, the collaborator and the adventurer. These "roles" are not confined to an individual learner, or a particular context; they *are not* learning styles, just ways of explaining how learners might "see themselves" in particular contexts and at particular times, and then learn accordingly. The learner decides how to interact, and act, within a learning activity. The question that I therefore focus on in this chapter is: How do learners identify and adopt different roles for their learning?

Recognising different understandings of learning

As I discussed in the earlier chapters, different theories of learning directly influence the role of the teacher, the role the learner takes and the way we think about knowledge. We also know that learners have a range of conceptualisations of learning and self-assessment, and that these are important in determining how and when they learn. But while teachers may adopt a particular theory of learning and *teach* accordingly, learners may have quite a different theory and *learn* accordingly. Although these differing views do not stop learners from learning, they do create situations of conflict and confusion when learners do not appear to "get it" or "do it" as the teacher envisioned. This situation can also create the illusion of learning when learners feel they need to "guess" what the teacher wants, or refrain from setting their own goals, in order to (as they see it), "play the game".

At times, both learners and teachers participate in the same paradigm but not necessarily to good effect. If a teacher believes that learning is about providing information, facts and "filling the brain", then learners might participate in learning to recall that information. Berry and Sahlberg (1996) identified learners' views of learning in the classroom as being about "transmission of information and reproducing memorized bits of it" (p. 34). Their claim was borne out by the students in the present study who held the less sophisticated views of learning. These students used practice as a strategy to reproduce facts, which was perhaps not surprising, given that school-based learning often rewards learners who are able to recall information in tidy, well-presented exercise books, an approach that often has little relevance to actual learning (learning categories A, B and C). As in Ramsden's (1988) work, the students were delivering what they thought the teacher would reward. Unfortunately, the problem for educators is that a student's success in terms of scores on his or her performance or assessments does not necessarily reflect real learning; rather, it better reflects that student's ability to memorise facts (Au, 2009).

True learning is what makes life worth living; by its very nature, learning invites an optimistic stance. It lets us believe that knowing about something in a new way contributes to our own and others' wellbeing. We want to learn, and we need to believe we can learn. Difficulties arise for young people when they do not see themselves as part of that process and cannot develop an identity of themselves as learners. As shown in Chapters 4 and 6, students, when formulating their views of learning or self-assessment, were influenced by the school setting. However, they also experienced learning and being learners in many other contexts. In part, school settings tend to make outcomes, rather than actual learning, important and real. Contrast this with learners in a judo class, an art class, engaged in a trampolining exercise who believe their learning enables them to achieve something both now and in the future. Setting goals for themselves is part of this exercise.

My point here is that learning and learners cannot be understood without reference to a context or an activity. Bruner's (1996) claim that "Learning, remembering, talking, imagining: all of them are made possible by participating in a culture" (p. xi) makes pertinent the need to examine context in relation to student learning. The multiple contexts in which we all participate contribute to our notions and experiences of learning, just as the ability to recognise the aspects of each context helps the "chameleonic learner" to know how and when to learn.

Keeping an eye on context

Chameleons can swivel each eye independently, enabling a 360 degree view and three-dimensional vision and thereby helping them catch prey and alerting them to danger. This aspect is represented in an old saying from the Malagasy people of Madagascar, who capture another vital aspect of context—connection between the past and the future: "Wise people are like the chameleon: They keep one eye on the past and one eye on the future" (Darling, 1997, p. 38). Simultaneously receiving two different images of the world is an inviting concept; one that would certainly support the concepts of keeping an "open mind" and multiple vision. Perhaps we could also say that wise learners are like chameleons: they keep one eye on the activity and one eye on themselves; moreover, the ability to "change colours" according to context while retaining a strong sense of self is as critical for the learner as it is for the chameleon.

While learning challenges our current knowledge, ability and expertise, it also supports a sense of identity of ourselves as learners. Children involved in skateboarding know what they want to achieve. Children attempting to ride a bike know what they want to achieve. But does a child in a mathematics class really know what she wants to achieve, and can she relate it to her learning? To create an enjoyable and exciting learning environment is not to make the work easy for the learner; it is to make the learner feel at ease with the challenge and his own role in it, to enable him to feel that sense of fulfilment in the small things he does.

Learning in a classroom setting needs to be "fun" to encourage a learner's active and intentional participation. This is particularly so for secondary schools, where learners who are not motivated and enthused stop engaging in the learning or choose to leave school. This does not mean teachers need to create fun-filled adventures in the classroom to compete with the learner's world outside school. Instead, students' imaginations and senses of fun can be maximised when they recognise and enjoy learning through roles within the classroom. I explain these roles more fully below, through the voices of the young people in this book, but first I want to consider how context mediates student role.

Context and student role

The results from my study on Year 7 and Year 8 students indicate that the *role* of the learner depends on the context in which learning and assessment take place; thus, the role the learner plays in any given setting is influenced by their conception of learning and self-assessment. For example, when learners primarily hold a less sophisticated conception of learning, their experiences and roles in learning are limited to replicating the material they are learning; they practise a skill until they master it, or they rote learn until they remember the facts. They are less inclined to utilise opportunities to learn through other roles.

The students in my study assumed various roles and responsibilities when they participated in learning and self-assessment activities. These roles were not directed or determined by teachers and came naturally to the students, who identified what they needed to achieve their goals, and how. Being keen observers, their choice of role was determined by the context for learning, their own goal and their needs.

Skilled teachers identify how students choose to interact with the learning content, and then determine how best to support each of these learners *in his or her role*. When this happens, learning occurs naturally and freely in a classroom setting, with the student-directed learning enabled by the teacher. Learners personalise their own learning in a meaningful and relevant way that is determined by their approach to their learning rather than necessarily what they are learning.

When learning is not relevant, students rely on conceptions of learning and self-assessment that promote a surface level of learning. For these students, learning is about recall, and self-assessment is based on another person telling them they have learnt. Some of the students in my study connected learning with the ability to remember rote-learn information: "Right, we'll call up the memory and they write it down on the paper inside your head." Another student attributed low marks in a test to a poor memory—not his poor understanding: "I'm losing my memory. I'm badder than I was." Even when their teacher gave a "memory cue", some students were unable to use, or later recall, the information if their understanding was not sufficient to apply that knowledge. I observed an incident when the teacher described a "braided river" as similar to a girl's braided plaits. When later asked about braided rivers in an assessment, the only information several students could recall was the girl's plaits. McCrudden and Corkill (2010) document this phenomenon in relation to reading. They found that learners who are distracted during their reading of a text with information that is novel but unrelated to the main idea can be "seduce[d] … towards this highly interesting, unimportant information at the expense of a passage's main ideas, thus interfering with learning" (p. 283).

The goal setter

The goal setter is an effective learning role because it clarifies learning outcomes for the learner and provides clear learning goals, thereby fostering the drive, commitment and motivation learners bring to an activity. By identifying their learning goals, learners focus on an activity in an intentional manner. The learner's agency and perceived point of learning thus affect how they approach the learning task. Also influential is the personal *goal* for learning. As Paley (1999) noted after years of working with young children, there is a "natural tendency of a young child to study, with great concentration, that which interests her at the moment" (p. 64).

For the students quoted in this book, learning goals were most often initiated by their teachers rather than by them. Teachers sometimes made the goal explicit, but many times they left it implicit in the form of assessment chosen to "measure" the learning. The students used this information, given either directly through the teacher or indirectly through classroom assessments, to identify the goal of the activity or what was important to learn. However, the students sometimes had other aims, which they used as the basis of their goals, such as when trampolining or learning a speech. Therefore, the level of ownership of the learning that the students assumed depended on who identified the goal (teacher, parent or student).

It was evident from my study that formulation of the goal also influences the role of the learner. Personalised learning occurs when *learners* deliberately set *their own* goals. Opportunity to do this is integral to self-assessment because when learners set personal goals they take more responsibility for their learning, they have a better appreciation of what they are trying to achieve and they develop the criteria to identify when they have learnt. They rely less on the teacher, parent, mark or grade to inform them they have learnt. They are also more motivated to learn when they choose their own learning goals and identify their own criteria for determining when they have achieved them.

Conversely, when a teacher sets the learning goals, some of the control that students enjoy diminishes. This lessening of control can be minimised by teachers ensuring their students clearly understand both the goals and the criteria for assessing their learning. So, while all learners may not always have the ability (initially) or opportunity to actively set their goals, they need to be encouraged to play some role in the process. When learners recognise their ability to meet externally set goals, they are more likely to be motivated to achieve. And when learners feel confident they can attain a goal, they *value* it. However, if they do not value the goal (as shown in the tepee example in Chapter 6), they are less likely to commit to that activity.

Self-assessment practices reinforce a learner's motivation for learning (Crooks, 2007; Tan, 2007). Results from this study highlight the importance of an active role for the student rather than the passive role of complying with the teacher's request. Within the school setting, students often self-assessed their work because their teacher had asked them to do this. As the students saw it, this was part of the teacher's requirements. They completed their self-assessment sheets with little reference to their learning. In contrast, the students who had clear learning goals, such as those in the trampolining class, could closely link their self-assessment to their learning, a situation consistent with the view that self-assessment is central to learning (Kozulin & Presseisen, 1995), and with the notion of sustainable assessment for lifelong learning (Boud & Falchikov, 2007; Tan, 2007). For each learner, assessment to understand learning needs to continue beyond formal assessment systems.

Learners who hold sophisticated conceptions of self-assessment actively set goals to assist their learning and formulate goals and criteria with which to measure their progress. This approach allows them to exercise more autonomy and responsibility for their learning. They rely less on teachers to identify that they have learnt, and they are more confident in their attempts to learn new skills because they have identified what these skills are within the framework of the teacher's goals. Take, for example, the student in my study who attempted a complex and difficult flip when trampolining. She could explain what she had to do and could execute parts of it, but not in a seamless movement. She *knew* what she was trying to achieve based on the teacher's instructions, and through observations of others who could do it, but her personal learning goals specific to this activity related to where she was on the continuum of learning the skills associated with the flip. She did not rely on the teacher to tell her what part of the manoeuvre she could or could not do because she could literally "feel" her learning through her execution of the movements within the flip.

The self-assessor

The self-assessor is an effective role because it enables learners to take responsibility for identifying when learning occurs and also for identifying the steps required for further learning (van Kraayenoord & Paris, 1997). Self-assessors place greater priority on establishing their goals and criteria for assessing their learning and less on teachers' marks or grades. The role of self-assessor is integral to learning because self-assessment enables learners to facilitate further learning. By self-assessing in a formative way, learners develop reflective thinking skills and can apply these to metacognitive learning strategies.

The influence of context relative to the self-assessor was highlighted in my study by students who self-assessed to satisfy teacher expectations (during class activities) and those who self-assessed in relation to their own learning goals (during judo, abseiling and while making a tepee). All teachers in the study required students to self-assess their work, but the students did not necessarily take on a self-assessor role when completing the prescribed self-assessment sheets. There were many instances within art, mathematics, social studies and food and nutrition lessons of students taking compliant, passive and submissive roles that were not conducive to reliable or valid self-assessments.

The self-assessment activities that I observed in the classrooms were often summative, as opposed to student-initiated, which were largely formative. When the students self-assessed their work within the formative assessment environment, their relationships with their peers and their teachers changed. For example, self-assessing as part of a formative assessment exercise tended to involve working closely with teachers and peers. This relationship between teacher and learner is a key differentiator of formative and summative assessment (Black & Wiliam, 2006; Crooks, 2007), and the shift in this relationship becomes important when self-assessment is incorporated into the curriculum. In response to the importance of this changing relationship, Wiliam (2006) draws attention to the need for teacher professional development to support teachers' understanding and use of formative assessment strategies. Perhaps more pressing, in order for assessment to have a formative component, is the need to understand how *learners* use assessment information. The question of whether the assessment data inform the *learner* is what ultimately establishes whether an assessment tool has a formative or a summative function.

In the present study, self-assessment in the school situation was structured so it had few formative elements. Two different forms of self-assessment were evident. One involved a formal structured process, usually initiated by the teacher in the form of worksheet-type activities where students fill in gaps, complete a sentence or make a mark on a continuum. However, the way the students completed these forms did not always indicate how they felt about their learning or performance but, rather, how they perceived the *function* of these self-assessment sheets, and their relative merits. The second type of self-assessment involved criteria created or developed by the students. This informal, personal self-assessment was, for the students, generally of a private nature and associated with the actual learning process or product. One of the key features of learner-initiated self-assessment is that it occurs at all stages of the learning process and tends to be a formative and fluid process, whereas teacher-directed self-assessment occurs at the *end* of a learning situation rather than during the learning activity and hence is largely a summative process.

The following example illustrates how learners can manipulate teacher-directed self-assessments. This observation took place during a food and nutrition lesson during which the students each cooked and ate a pie. After the students had finished eating, their teacher gave them a structured self-assessment sheet and asked them to self-assess their pies in relation to four factors—appearance, flavour, texture and presentation. The following extract from this observation highlights a situation in which learners really do not know why they self-assess or how it affects their learning. They view it as another process of the teaching session, and as another "hoop" to jump through, rather than as a means to learn:

> *Teacher showing class the self-assessment sheets on an OHT. Learners paying attention and sitting at their desks. The self-assessment sheets have questions attached to assist the student. There is a scale of 1–3 for rating success (3 listed as being awesome). Chris helping teacher hand out self-assessment sheets. Chris going through his self-assessment sheet...*
>
> *Boy sits next to Chris and asks him how to fill out the self-assessment sheet against the four headings. Chris says, 'Just write a comment.' Boy says, 'Oh, you mean ... just ... good.' Chris says, 'Yeah, but don't just go good, good, good, good.'*
>
> *Boy (and me wondering): 'Why not?'*
>
> *Chris: 'Because you get told off for not thinking.'*

Another student, John, responded in a "jokey" way, a little like the deviant comedy to please peers that I described in Chapter 2.

CRITERIA	JOHN'S RESPONSES
Appearance:	Was a big pie
Flavour:	Soil
Texture:	Hard
Presentation:	Bad

At the time of this observation, I wondered what happened to the self-evaluations, and whether the teacher read them, and so asked John about them. John had made a particularly big and cumbersome-looking pie, with dry, thick pastry, hence his evaluation that the texture was hard. Nonetheless, he did manage to eat the pie, thus removing any evidence. This extract concerns the presentation:

John was finding it hard to comment on presentation. When he put down 'bad', I asked him what happened to these self-assessment sheets. For instance, did they go on the school report? He looked worried and said, 'I don't know, should I ask?' I said to him, 'Oh, I just wondered whether you knew what happened to these ... why do you do them?' John looks at his sheet and got his rubber out. He rubs out the word bad. And changes it to 'a good effort'. He looked up at me and said, 'I did it the way the teacher told me to do it. It just came out that way.' I then asked him whether my comments about the report helped him change his mind. He screws up his face and said, 'Yeah.'

The questions I asked John had a marked effect on his responses when he considered the consequences of completing the self-assessment, and when he thought the teacher might use these in her own evaluation. Some months later, when I collected up work samples, I observed another subtle change on John's pie evaluation sheet. He had changed the word "soil" to describe the flavour of the pie to "lingering". The food and nutrition teacher had written in her comments on the work sample, noting, "Good work John. Congratulations on your pie." The teacher had neither sampled nor examined the pie.

When the students in my study assigned themselves grades as a result of self-assessment in the classroom, they tended to give themselves average marks to avoid either "skiting" or putting themselves down (as described in Chapter 6), and they were clearly influenced by their perceptions of the type of responses teachers expected. Consequently, these self-assessment techniques were little more than self-marking exercises. They were neither true indicators of what the students believed represented their work, nor were they based on any criteria for determining the outcome of the learning. Given that there are "two key elements in classrooms where students appeared to be highly motivated: formative evaluation and student self-management" (Benson, 2000, p. 30), it is particularly important that learners are encouraged to self-assess their learning based on their own or pre-established criteria. The self-assessor is a critical role for the student, but not when that role is so clearly teacher-prescribed. These two elements (self-directed learning and formative assessment) are greatly enhanced through teacher feedback. As Crooks (2010) recently advised teachers, "students will be supported and encouraged as their learning progresses through helpful feedback from the teachers, peers, and family. Such *assessment for learning* has been shown to be far more valuable for students than any formal testing or reporting" (p. 4).

I noted two key differences between the way learners experience assessment practices in school settings and out-of-school settings. In structured out-of-school settings the system of assessment is prescriptive and learners are provided with role models of advanced performances. Learners who attend learning activities in community-based out-of-school settings have access to expert models and their learning goals are usually embedded in the activities. These goals include acquisition of medals, badges or belts, and inclusion in performances for competitions, examinations and exhibitions. For example, in judo, all learners work towards the next colour belt and therefore the moves they are learning and on which they are being assessed are based on the curriculum for that belt. The class includes learners with white, yellow, orange, blue and brown belts, so even young novices can see—literally—where they are headed. On netball courts, children of primary school age play netball alongside secondary school and adult players. These situations exemplify another context that provides learners with opportunities to develop their expertise in self-assessment. For these learners, external rewards do not encourage self-assessment practices; opportunity to observe and work alongside peers and models does.

The more sophisticated and inclusive the conceptions of self-assessment, the more likely learners are to involve themselves intentionally in goal setting focused on the desired outcome. They depend less on teachers to know they have learnt, and they rely less on norm-referenced tests. Instead, they use criteria first established by the teacher (self-assessment category D) and later by themselves (self-assessment category E) to determine whether learning has occurred. This evaluation also tends not to be public statements on paper about their work but something they think about or conduct privately.

The peer teacher

The peer teacher is an effective learning role because it enables the learners who "teach" or "explain" to clarify their own understanding. In a sense, the role of the peer teacher requires metacognitive skills that enhance learning. Many learners take on the role of sharing their information, skills or expertise with their peers; in my study, it was usually friends who chose to assist and work with one another. Even when learners believe they have not mastered a particular activity, they are willing to contribute their understanding of the task to assist another. This was apparent in both the within-school and out-of-school settings in my study, although there was a fundamental difference between the two settings.

In the school setting, situations in which students helped teach their peers tended to be informal and peer-initiated. Nevertheless, the peer teachers typically took the responsibility seriously and attempted to explain or demonstrate the desired outcome for the other learner. While this interaction had benefits for the peer receiving the advice or explanation, it was likely to be equally beneficial for the peer providing the explanation. As Brandt (1994) identifies, learners improve their own understanding when teaching a peer. Nuthall (1999, 2007) also found that the private talk of learners in a classroom setting frequently relates to task requirements and plays a marked role in their learning.

In the out-of-school settings in my study, it was usual for an older peer, or a peer with more expertise and experience in the activity, to be informally involved in teaching the younger peer the activity. This occurred mostly while the learners were engaged in an activity where one had more mastery than the other of a particular skill, such as a throw in judo, a double flip in trampolining, a dance movement. The interaction and involvement between peers became more of an apprenticeship role—one that demonstrated "the centrality of activity in learning and knowledge and highlight[ed] the inherently context-dependent, situated and enculturating nature of learning" (Brown, Collins, & Duguid, 1989, p. 39).

Vygotsky's (1978, 1981, 1988) theory proposes learners can be encouraged to a deeper level of understanding when working with more knowledgeable peers. A New Zealand study conducted by Borg and McDrury (1996) provides confirmation for this claim. The researchers found that peer teaching led, for the peer teachers, to positive gains in both cognitive learning and the facilitation of social skills (Borg & McDrury, 1996). In the present study, it was evident that peer support advantaged both the learning and self-assessment processes. In both school and out-of-school settings, the learners ranged in ability and age, and it was this diversity that the students recognised and used when providing assistance to their peers, or requesting it. Peers and siblings regularly "translated" teacher and parent concepts. The students assisted one another, modelled from one another and taught one another in a variety of contexts such as mathematics, dancing, abseiling and public speaking. For teachers, encouraging peer teaching is worthwhile, both for the gains students can make by teaching and the gains they can make by learning from the language their peers use.

In many learning contexts, learners are keen observers and utilise the idea of a "peer teacher" to their own advantage. In a judo session that I observed, the learners in the class were working on their forward and backward rolls, and each could see his or her peers working on these movements. The young judo learners heard "grunting" sounds (generated by a release of air through the execution of the movement) that the older learners made informally and seemingly automatically when they executed a backward roll. The young learners tried to model this sound whenever they attempted a backward roll, but their sounds and their movements often did not connect. In this example, it is evident that these younger learners are coming to learn about this movement:

6.30 p.m. The group are now in a line practising backward and forward rolls. They have to do three backward rolls and then join the back of the line. After they have gone through these a couple of times, they then do forward rolls. It seems that when they do backward rolls they make a sort of sound. A loud grunt. The adults make a lot of noise associated with their roll, and the children seem to copy. The children are making the noise because it is seen as part of the movement. They imitate the sound but do not seem to have connected it with the movement. Some make the sound before they attempt the backward roll. Perhaps the first part of learning something like this is in the doing rather than the knowing.

The peer assessor

In contrast to the peer teacher, peer assessors tend to examine their peer's work or activity and offer suggestions in relation to the other's work. They do not demonstrate or explain the activity at hand, but rather use the peer's work as a basis for discussion. The peer assessor is an effective role because it provides the peer who offers the advice with an opportunity to reframe and discuss the perceived goals. It also provides the learner with another interpretation of the activity. For learners receiving advice from their peers, the attention they give to their performance is enhanced through having their peers mediate their self-assessment.

There was evidence in my study to suggest that the students found peer assessment a helpful process in self-assessing their own work because they often sought feedback from one another while they were working. But the extent to which peer assessment was useful in promoting learning seemed to depend on who instigated the assessment and what type of assessment was used.

Peer assessment was evident in my study in two forms within the school setting. The first was teacher-initiated and teacher-directed peer assessments, and the second was informal peer assessments initiated by the students and therefore closely associated with their learning. In the classroom, peer assessment took place in semiformal situations, but it was during informal peer assessment that students assumed the unique role of assessing peers' work in relation to either teacher-initiated or peer-established criteria.

In this study, when teachers constructed the peer assessments, they designed them to reflect specific areas to be assessed. These assessments generally required learners to assign marks or grades and so tended to be quantitative in nature. But although the students knew why they were to provide a mark or grade, they had no specific criteria on which to make a judgement about the areas identified for assessment. And even when criteria were supplied, the students assessing their peers tended to ignore these—and sometimes even the marks or scores they had assigned—and to rely on other factors, such as their attitudes towards the student they were assessing.

During an observation involving a speech competition, I noted peers being asked to assess one another's performance. Each was given a list of areas on which to base the decision regarding the allocated mark. While the students used the assessment sheet that outlined the areas, such as purpose, introduction and content, it became evident that they also chose to alter decisions if their own intuitive judgement did not match the scores they awarded their peer. The overall aim of grading the performances was to choose the three best learners to enter the school speech competition. The students were supposed to mark one another on the basis of performance and ability, but other variables such as friendship and popularity generally had a stronger influence. When Deb, who features in this example, is asked by her teacher to put forward the names for the finals, she does not "go by the score":

Each student has a turn at reading their speech to the rest of the class. The students have a sheet of paper in front of them with room for student name and 6 columns for grades. Each column and grade represented a part of the speech. They were: Purpose (5); Introduction (10); Content (30); Delivery (30); Conclusion (10); and Reaction (15), followed by a total score.

Jane gives her speech. She writes her name on the board so the other students can write her name on their sheet. She speaks quickly and relies on her cue cards. Some words are mumbled. John's score for Jane is 3 8 28 22 7 10 (78).

A boy gives a speech immediately after and John scores him 5 9 29 29 9 14 (95). John uses a calculator to work out the final score.

Deb is giving her speech now. She is confident and makes little use of her cards. John's score for Deb is 4 9 22 25 9 14. He adds it up twice to make sure of the final score. His calculator both times says 90 but he then writes down 74. (The actual score should be 83.)

The students are then asked by the teacher to select two peers they think should be represented in the finals. I watch Deb make her choice and then ask her how she decided. She says, 'I had to choose two, but I didn't go by the score. I scored them too highly yesterday so I decided to score lower today.'

In the next example, the students were in a social studies class and their teacher had asked them to comment on and grade their peers' work, in this case a presentation featuring a model of a river and an accompanying explanatory speech. The teacher also asked the students to evaluate their own presentation in their "home sample books", exercise books where samples of student work are collated over time, and to select parts of the peer assessment to include in that evaluation. The following extract shows that while Deb found the comments made by peers more useful than grades, Marie included the grades because she was proud of them:

I notice that the learners have chosen particular pieces of peer evaluations from the peer evaluation exercise. I take samples of these to illustrate what they have chosen for their evaluations, and also how they have evaluated another person. In their home sample books, they have included the peer evaluations under the heading, 'These people in my class have made these comments about my work.' They could select out of all the class comments what they wanted to include. They had presented their river model to the class, and each class member had to write a comment and give a grade. For example, a peer comment to Marie was 'well done and don't say it's dumb ... have original ideas some labels aren't right'. Marie had also included the scores the peers had given her (e.g., 8/10 and 4/5). When I looked at Deb's work, she had not included the scores. I ask Marie why she had included scores in her work. She said she was proud of them, while Deb said she didn't include the scores because the comments were more interesting for her.

This extract also shows that learners do not always value peer feedback or want particular types of feedback. A study undertaken by Sadler and Good (2006) suggests that peer grading should not be equated with peer teaching. According to the authors, "self-grading appears to result in increased student learning; peer-grading does not" (p. 1).

The second type of peer assessment involved assessment initiated informally by the student. In contrast to the summative teacher-directed peer assessment, it was generally a formative process. Informal peer assessment had an impact on student learning because it generally occurred during an activity and contributed to how the student undertook the task. The following extract illustrates how learners informally initiate comments on and talk to one another about their work, including their interpretation of what they are expected to do. Often, learners provide feedback to their peers in situations where they believe they have something to offer, even when (as noted in the following example) such advice is not sought. In this extract, the students are in an art class and are working on their pieces of art on the floor:

> One girl has just told another boy, 'It would be easier if you did bigger houses.' Then she tells Peter, 'You're not meant to colour in, you're meant to rub it in.' Peter looks worried and looks over to her work. The art method was supposed to fill in the centre of the house with pastel and then rub it in to give it a blurred or smudged effect. He was colouring it in block style. This was an interesting episode given that this girl was monitoring her own and others' work, making comparisons and providing feedback. Girl then sees that Peter looks concerned as he tries to remove some of the pastel with a ruler, and says to him, 'Don't worry. It'll be OK.' Peter is still trying to scratch off excess pastel from his picture.

Later, while I was having morning tea with the art teacher, she discussed with me her role in the art lesson. She agreed that peers learn from one another, by looking at and asking questions about their work, and she encouraged her students to do this. She said students often ask one another questions, such as "How did you do that?" and "What are you doing?" She observed that peer assessment is informal and cannot be planned.

Of particular interest in this study was that in no case did assessors ask the peers they were assessing what their goals were or what they were attempting to achieve. Therefore, the assessments occurred within the framework of understanding held by the peer assessor, rather than by the learner. At times, the learner was assisted because the peer assessor more clearly understood what the teacher was requesting. For example, during an art session, a peer assessor carefully explained a particular technique to a classmate because she had assessed the classmate's work as not following directions about using pastels. She helped the student improve his artwork with respect to the teacher's criteria for "success" but did not ask her classmate what effect he was attempting to achieve with his pastels.

Although the teachers in my study sometimes asked students to assess their peers' work, this was usually less successful for learning than the informal peer assessments. Admittedly, the peer assessors allowed qualities such as friendship, popularity and other social aspects to influence their assessments of their peers. However, when peers actively sought or provided one another with advice or opinions, the process seemed generally beneficial for the students because of the types of questions they asked of one another. This is what Sperling (1993) found in her study of peer assessment amongst fourth graders in the United States. "Sometimes," said Sperling, "a student's most probing thinking occurs during an assessment session with a peer" (p. 75).

The collaborator

The collaborator is an effective role because it enables learners to work together on a common learning goal. Collaborative problem solving is an effective learning process because it emphasises the support and skills of others when working together (Matusov et al., 2002). Some learners scaffold difficult concepts for their peers through collaboration and, by so doing, work within a framework of a community of learners (Lave, 1996; Matusov et al., 2002). Regardless of the sophistication of their views of learning, the students in the study tended to work with others to achieve their goals. This was evident in activities within the classroom, such as mathematics and writing stories, and in out-of-school contexts, such as judo, abseiling and dancing. The students who feared a new activity, such as abseiling or attempting a mathematics problem, utilised their peers' experiences and support when undertaking the new task. The students who collaborated successfully were acting neither as peer assessors nor peer teachers. They encouraged, cajoled and offered advice to support their friends. Collaboration encouraged more students to become active participants in the learning process. As Vygotsky (1978) commented when identifying the centrality of others to his theory of the zone of proximal development, learners develop "in collaboration with more capable peers" (p. 86). In this study, collaborating with others seemed a natural process for the students, although they did this in different ways.

The students sometimes collaborated in establishing the goals of the learning, or the intended focus of the task. For example, during a mathematics lesson, one student asked, "What are we meant to be doing?", and others in her group explained the intent of the activity. In school situations such as a mathematics class, the students supported one another as they attempted to solve problems irrespective of whether this was the teacher's intention. They collaborated in other activities such as sports, speech making, food and nutrition, art and any activity where peers were involved in the general setting.

Earlier studies examining collaboration amongst learners established that the communities in which learners participate (both at home and school) influence their propensity to collaborate (Matusov et al., 2002; Rogoff & Toma, 1997). In a study that examined collaboration amongst learners, Rogoff and Toma (1997) found that whether parents and teachers exposed learners to a transmission model or a participation model of instruction depended on their parents' and teachers' modes of instruction. These modes, in turn, were strongly influenced by the parents' and the teachers' sociocultural settings. While Rogoff and Toma were not arguing for an "either/or" approach to assisting learners, they made the point that communities influence the mode of instruction. They also observed that as communities change, so too does the mode.

In the present study, learning contexts that encouraged collaboration with others included judo, dancing and sports because the learners did not participate in these activities alone. These settings also facilitated the students working together collaboratively because, within a team or an activity, a spirit of cooperation rather than competition was encouraged. As the students within these contexts became familiar with collaboration, some of them attempted to use these strategies at school. On some occasions, teachers discouraged collaboration—for example, during individual mathematics work or when taking tests—but at other times they encouraged it; for example, during art or food and nutrition classes.

The adventurer

The adventurer role is marked by risk taking—moving beyond the safe boundaries of what the learner can do—and it was most evident in the study during practical activities such as abseiling, judo and trampolining, and during conceptual learning activities such as solving mathematical problems. The students with the most sophisticated conceptions of learning (learning categories D and E) and self-assessment (self-assessment categories D, E and F) were the students most likely to see learning as an adventure.

The adventurer is an effective role because of this characteristic of allowing students to take risks when learning. Creating contexts for risk taking is particularly important in encouraging learners to move away from viewing schools as institutions that provide rote-learning and intellectually limiting instruction (Moll & Whitmore, 1993). Learners with a less sophisticated conception of learning (e.g., filling up the brain, memorising and reproducing) will continue to view learning as the mere transmission of information unless actively encouraged to be adventurous in their learning.

The ability to take risks in learning is important when approaching and undertaking new tasks. The daily challenges that learners face necessitate sophisticated self-assessment skills to identify the requirements of the task and the skills they bring to it. This aspect of learning is a critical role for the learner and one that contributes to the overall context for successful learning.

Some evidence in the present study suggested the role of the adventurer was stifled or discouraged by school assessment systems that encouraged the "right" answer or a narrow way of thinking. The students quickly identified when teachers asked a question but already had an answer in mind, which resulted in the game of determining what the teacher wanted. When learners are not adventurous in their learning, they end up comparing themselves with peers and examining individual differences rather than focusing on their learning.

Certainly, the students were more active in out-of-school contexts when it came to goal setting and using pre-established or personally identified criteria to ascertain whether learning had occurred. In these cases, rather than attempting to deliver what might be rewarded, the students attempted to perform activities based on their own goals and expectations; thus, these learners were more prepared to take risks to achieve their goals. This is an important factor in respect of further learning. Students need to know and feel both within school and out that they can take risks, even if it means giving incorrect answers or not doing something "right the first time" (Alton-Lee & Nuthall, 1992; Nuthall, 2007).

Self-assessment: Awareness of learning

The relationship between learning and self-assessment is dialogical; each process influences the other. Thus, the students in the study who held relatively unsophisticated conceptions of learning also held relatively unsophisticated conceptions of self-assessment, and vice versa. Students who experienced learning as the acquisition of skills or the recall of information (learning categories A and B) also conceptualised self-assessment as requiring external sources (self-assessment categories A and B) to verify they had learnt. Students holding more sophisticated views of learning (learning categories D and E) were more likely to actively develop criteria for self-assessment and to set goals to assess their learning (self-assessment categories D and E) than to rely on teachers or grades to confirm it (self-assessment categories A and B). In short, a student's conceptualisation of learning related inextricably to their conceptualisation of self-assessment because the two phenomena are aspects of a greater phenomenon—awareness of learning.

Variation in the experiences of learning and self-assessment demonstrates how these categories of description are likely to affect the way learners *approach* learning rather than their performance or outcome of learning. Results from the participating students' Progressive Achievement Tests (PATs) and classroom-based assessments indicated that students with a less sophisticated view of learning were not necessarily performing at a lower level than their peers. This finding confirms earlier research investigating the learning of Years 7 and 8 students in science and social studies: "students whose percentile scores on school-administered PAT tests indicate very high levels of ability appear to learn in exactly the same way as students whose percentile scores are relatively low" (Nuthall, 1996, p. 2).

What does this tell us? First, performance on tests and other school-based assessment tasks is not a good indicator of *how* learners learn nor of the motivation learners bring to the learning. This has already been documented at both primary and secondary school levels (Broadfoot et al., 1991; Nash, 1997). However, the data from the present study show that the ways learners conceptualise learning and self-assessment affect their approach to a task. If they believe learning is largely about memorising and reproducing, they will adopt strategies to facilitate this type of learning. Even those learners who perform well on PAT and other tests will approach learning in this superficial way if they have a less sophisticated conception of learning.

When assessment procedures used in a school setting focus on recall of knowledge rather than on understanding, learners can be inhibited from striving for understanding, meaning and purpose in their learning. Moreover, the way in which school and classroom systems reward certain forms of learning suggests learners are, in effect, encouraged to take a less sophisticated conception of learning. The development of students' reflective skills is hindered because surface approaches to assessment correspondingly encourage an atomistic and surface approach to learning (Crooks, 1988; Gipps, 1994; Ramsden, 1988). Some students focus on getting the "right" answer, quickly, at the expense of creativity and problem solving because it is rewarded through the school assessment system. A change in focus to problem-solving solutions may result in a range of answers, some better than others, and may encourage learners to think more laterally.

Conceptions of learning and self-assessment are hierarchical, but are neither static nor linear. Therefore, depending on the context, a student could hold several conceptions of learning and self-assessment. For example, they might express a higher conception of learning when discussing cricket techniques and learning about stance in cricket, but revert to a lower level of conception of learning when expressing experiences of rote-learning multiplication tables during a mathematics class at school. In general, in my study, the school-based conception of learning tended to predominate. However, students holding the least sophisticated view were unlikely to see either learning or self-assessment in more inclusive and sophisticated ways, and were therefore less likely to hold more than one conception. Students who demonstrated a sophisticated conception of learning or self-assessment could demonstrate less sophisticated views when describing particular contexts. Research in the 1990s argued that learners operate in several systems and need to be flexible in their approach to learning (Boaler, 1993; Rogoff & Toma, 1997); some learners adapt even their conceptions of learning and self-assessment according to context, and this in turn influences the way they approach the task. In effect, they become chameleonic learners.

The influence of context: The chameleonic effect

The dialectical relationship between the individual and the social group drove Vygotsky's theory on learning and development. Such a relationship was evident within the present study, where the environment influenced the students and they equally influenced their environment. The critical relationship between context and the learner is also evident in the work of many educators who take a sociocultural approach to their educational research and theory (e.g., Filer & Pollard, 1996; Lave, 1996; Pollard, 1997; Rogoff, 2003). As Gipps (1994) identified, "context has a crucial role in both learning and assessment" (p. 166).

Clearly, context affects how students approach a learning task. However, the context also depends on how the learners perceive it because the context consists partly of the learners' perceptions of the activity and the cultural components of that activity. Therefore, the activity, or the task itself (whether it is a learning or self-assessment task), depends on both student conceptions of learning and the context in which it occurs. Thus, two factors in particular contribute to the different ways learners approach learning or self-assessment activities: their conceptions of learning and self-assessment, and the contexts within which that learning occurs.

Both the ethnographic and phenomenographic phases of my research showed some students placing greater value on teacher feedback while self-assessing their work and others placing more value on their own beliefs about their work. In particular, students who held less sophisticated conceptions of learning and self-assessment were more likely to require support from teachers while self-assessing their work. These students were also inclined to talk about self-assessment in relation to presentation and appearance of "work" rather than in relation to their performance or learning associated with that task. They were more likely to focus on discrete, assigned learning tasks, rather than the "bigger picture". The students' conceptions of learning and self-assessment influenced how they perceived the learning task, and therefore how they approached it. For teachers to facilitate further learning for these students, the focus must be on changing learners' *conceptions* rather than changing the activity.

The learners in this book showed how they immersed themselves in their learning and made sense of these experiences as they negotiated the worlds of school and beyond. For them, learning was a natural part of their own understanding of the world; they recognised that sometimes their learning was measured as "outcomes" by others and sometimes by themselves; that some learning appears to be given greater worth by others, and other learning valued more by themselves. Here we have the chameleonic learner—learners who learn in multiple environments, adapting and changing, influenced by their own values, beliefs and motivations, according to their aspirations and the boundaries they, and others, set. Freedom of learning lies in knowing that, in any context, in any setting and in any group, learning enables learners to be who they want to be. Each learner chooses his or her colour and identity. These are always an approximate, always negotiated and always open to the possibilities of a life imagined.

References

Alton-Lee, A., & Nuthall, G. (1992). A generative methodology for classroom research. *Educational Philosophy and Theory*, 24(2), 29–55.

Andrade, H. G. (2000). Using rubrics to promote thinking and learning. *Educational Leadership*, 57(5), 13–19.

Anthony, G. (1994). *Learning strategies in mathematics education*. Unpublished doctoral dissertation, Massey University, Palmerston North.

Au, W. (2009). *Unequal by design: High-stakes testing and the standardization of inequality*. New York: Routledge.

Barr, M. A. (2000). Looking at the learning record. *Educational Leadership*, 57(5), 20–24.

Benson, S. H. (2000). Make mine an A. *Educational Leadership*, 57(5), 30–33.

Berndt, T. J., & Keefe, K. (1992). Friends' influence on adolescents' perceptions of themselves at school. In D. H. Schunk & J. L. Meece (Eds.), *Student perceptions in the classroom* (pp. 51–73). Hillsdale, NJ: Lawrence Erlbaum.

Berry, J., & Sahlberg, P. (1996). Investigating pupils' ideas of learning. *Learning and Instruction*, 6(1), 19–36.

Biggs, J. (2003). *Teaching for quality learning at university*. Maidenhead: Open University Press.

Billett, S. (1996). Situated learning: Bridging sociocultural and cognitive theorising. *Learning and Instruction*, 6(3), 261–280.

Bishop, R., & Berryman, M. (2006). *Culture speaks: Cultural relationships and classroom learning*. Wellington: Huia.

Black, P. (1993). Formative and summative assessment by teachers. *Studies in Science Education*, 21, 49–97.

Black, P. (1994). Performance assessment and accountability: The experience in England and Wales. *Educational Evaluation and Policy Analysis*, 16(2), 191–203.

Black, P. (1998). Learning, league tables and national assessment: Opportunity lost or hope deferred? *Oxford Review of Education*, 24(1), 57–86.

Black, P., Harrison, C., Lee, C., Marshall, B., & Wiliam, D. (2003). *Assessment for learning: Putting it into practice*. Buckingham: Open University Press.

Black, P., & Wiliam, D. (2006). Developing a theory of formative assessment. In J. Gardner (Ed.), *Assessment and learning* (pp. 81–100). London: Sage.

Boaler, J. (1993). The role of contexts in the mathematics classroom: Do they make mathematics more "real"? *For the Learning of Mathematics*, 13(2), 12–17.

Borg, G., & McDrury, J. (1996, June). *Validity in group assessment*. Paper presented at the International Symposium on Validity in Educational Assessment, Otago University, Dunedin.

Boud, D., & Falchikov, N. (Eds.). (2007). *Rethinking assessment in higher education: Learning for the long term*. London: Routledge.

Boulton-Lewis, M. M., Marton, F., Lewis, D. C., & Wilss, L. A. (2000). Learning in formal and informal contexts: Conceptions and strategies of Aboriginal and Torres Strait Islander university students. *Learning and Instruction, 10*, 393–414.

Bourke, R. (1996, December). *But is it right? Students' conceptions of assessment*. Paper presented at the New Zealand Association for Research in Education (NZARE) conference, Nelson.

Bourke, R. (2000). *Students' conceptions of learning and self-assessment in context*. Doctoral dissertation, Massey University, Palmerston North.

Bourke, R., & Willis, D. (1998, July). *Teachers' use of assessment: Changing practices, changing minds*. Paper presented at the National Assessment Hui Aro Matawai, Christchurch.

Brandt, R. (1994). On making sense: A conversation with Magdalene Lampert. *Educational Leadership, 51*(5), 28–30.

Broadfoot, P. (1979). Communication in the classroom: A study of the role of assessment in motivation. *Educational Review, 31*(1), 3–10.

Broadfoot, P. (1996). Assessment and learning: Power or partnership? In H. Goldstein & T. Lewis (Eds.), *Assessment: Problems, developments and statistical issues* (pp. 21–40). London: John Wiley.

Broadfoot, P. (2000). Assessment and intuition. In T. Atkinson & G. Claxton (Eds.), *The intuitive practitioner: On the value of not always knowing what one is doing* (pp. 199–219). Buckingham: Open University Press.

Broadfoot, P., Abbott, D., Croll, P., Osborn, M., Pollard, A., & Towler, L. (1991). Implementing national assessment: Issues for primary teachers. *Cambridge Journal of Education, 21*(2), 153–168.

Brown, J. S., Collins, A., & Duguid, P. (1989). Situated cognition and the culture of learning. *Educational Researcher, 16*(1), 32–42.

Bruner, J. (1973). *The relevance of education*. New York: W. W. Norton.

Bullough, R. V. (2007). Ali: Becoming a student—a life history. In D. Thiessen & A. Cook-Sather (Eds.), *International handbook of student experience in elementary and secondary school* (pp. 493–516). Dordrecht: Springer.

Bullough, R. V. (2008). The writing of teachers' lives—where personal troubles and social issues meet. *Teacher Education Quarterly, Fall*, 5–24.

Campbell, E. (2003). *The ethical teacher*. Maidenhead: Open University Press.

Carle, E. (1984). *The mixed-up chameleon*. New York: Crowell.

Ceci, S. J., & Roazzi, A. (1994). The effects of context on cognition: Postcards from Brazil. In R. J. Sternberg & R. K. Wagner (Eds.), *Mind in context. Interactionist perspectives on human intelligence* (pp. 74–104). Cambridge: Cambridge University Press.

Chavajay, P., & Rogoff, B. (1999). Cultural variation in management of attention by children and their caregivers. *Developmental Psychology, 35*, 1079–1090.

Cook-Sather, A. (2007). Translating researchers: Re-imagining the work of investigating students' experiences in school. In D. Thiessen & A. Cook-Sather (Eds.), *International handbook of student experience in elementary and secondary school* (pp. 829–872). Dordrecht: Springer.

Cowley, J. (2008). *A letter from Joy Cowley*. Retrieved from http://www.joycowley.com/letter18.shtml

Crooks, T. J. (1988). The impact of classroom evaluation practices on students. *Review of Educational Research, 58*(4), 438–481.

Crooks, T. J. (2006, April). *Excellence in assessment for accountability purposes*. Paper presented at the EARLI SIG assessment conference, Chicago.

Crooks, T. J. (2007, April). *Key factors in the effectiveness of assessment for learning*. Paper presented at the annual meeting of the American Educational Research Association, Chicago.

Crooks, T. J. (2010). *Comments about implementing national standards*. Unpublished paper. Educational Assessment Research Unit, University of Otago.

Dall'Alba, G. (1994). Reflections on some faces of phenomenography. In J. A. Bowden & E. Walsh (Eds.), *Phenomenographic research: Variations in method. The Warburton symposium* (pp. 73–88). Melbourne: Royal Melbourne Institute of Technology.

Darling, K. (1997). *Chameleons on location*. New York: Lothrop, Lee & Shepard Books.

Daugherty, R., & Ecclestone, K. (2006). In J. Gardner (Ed.), *Assessment and learning* (pp. 149–167). London: Sage.

Deakin Crick, R., Broadfoot, P., & Claxton, G. (2004). Developing an effective lifelong learning inventory: The ELLI project. *Assessment in Education, 11*(3), 247–272.

Department for Education and Skills. (2006). *2020 Vision: Report of the Teaching and Learning in 2020 Review Group*. Retrieved from www.publications.teachernet.gov.uk/eorderingdownload/6856-DfEs-Teaching520and 520Learning.pdf

Donaldson, M. (1978). *Children's minds*. London: Fontana Press.

Drummond, M. J. (1993). *Assessing children's learning*. London: David Fulton.

Dyson, A. H. (2007). School literacy and the development of a child culture: Written remnants of the "gusto of life". In D. Thiessen & A. Cook-Sather (Eds.), *International handbook of student experience in elementary and secondary school* (pp. 115–142). Dordrecht: Springer.

Earl, L., & Katz, S. (2008). Getting to the core of learning: Using assessment for self-monitoring and self-regulation. In S. Swaffield (Ed.), *Unlocking assessment: Understanding for reflection and application* (pp. 90–104). London: Routledge.

Ecclestone, K. (2007). Learning assessment: Students' experiences in post-school qualifications. In D. Boud & N. Falchikov (Eds.), *Rethinking assessment in higher education: Learning for the long term* (pp. 41–54). London: Routledge.

Education Review Office. (2009). *Creating pathways and building lives: CPaBL in action. An evaluation.* Retrieved from http://www.minedu.govt.nz/ NZEducation/EducationPolicies/Schools/Initiatives/CPaBLCreatingPathwaysAndBuildingLives/FinalReportsCPaBLProject.aspx

Eisner, E. W. (1998). *The enlightened eye: Qualitative inquiry and the enhancement of educational practice*. Upper Saddle River, NJ: Merrill.

Eisner, E. W. (2000). Those who ignore the past ...: 12 'easy' lessons for the next millennium. *Journal of Curriculum Studies, 32*(2), 343–357.

Entwistle, N. (1987). A model of the teaching–learning process. In J. T. E. Richardson, M. W. Eysenck, & D. W. Piper (Eds.), *Student learning: Research in education and cognitive psychology* (pp. 13–28). Milton Keynes: Society for Research into Higher Education & Open University Press.

Filer, A. (1997). "At least they were laughing": Assessment and the functions of children's language in their 'news' session. In A. Pollard, D. Thiessen, & A. Filer (Eds.), *Children and their curriculum: The perspectives of primary and elementary school children* (pp. 81–98). London: Falmer Press.

Filer, A., & Pollard, A. (1996, September). *Assessment and career in a primary school*. Paper presented at the annual conference of the British Educational Research Association, Lancaster University, Lancaster.

Foucault, M. (1977). *Discipline and punish*. Harmondsworth: Penguin.

Gallagher, K., & Lortie, P. (2007). Building theories of their lives: Youth engaged in drama research. In D. Thiessen & A. Cook-Sather (Eds.), *International handbook of student experience in elementary and secondary school* (pp. 405–438). Dordrecht: Springer.

Gardner, H. (1991). *The unschooled mind: How children think and how schools should teach*. New York: Basic Books.

Garrison, J. (1997). *Dewey and Eros: Wisdom and desire in the art of teaching*. New York: Teachers College Press.

Gipps, C. V. (1994). *Beyond testing: Towards a theory of educational assessment*. London: Falmer Press.

Gipps, C., & Tunstall, P. (1998). Effort, ability and the teacher: Young children's explanations for success and failure. *Oxford Review of Education*, 24(2), 149–165.

Gleason, B. (2000). Pay for performance. *Educational Leadership*, 57(5), 82–83.

Graham, J. (2008). Rating the rankings. Australia. *AEU News*. Retrieved from http://www.aeuvic.asn.au/publications/files/News_1_Study.pdf

Greene, T. (2006). *There is more to education than exams*. Retrieved from http://www.independent.co.uk/opinion/commentators/tom-greene-there-is-more-to-education-than-exams-412171.html

Guerra, J. C., & Farr, M. (2002). Writing on the margins: The spiritual and autobiographical discourse of two Mexicanas in Chicago. In G. Hull & K. Schultz (Eds.), *School's out! Bridging out-of-school literacies with classroom practice* (pp. 96–123). New York: Teachers College Press.

Hager, P., & Halliday, J. (2006). *Recovering informal learning*. Dordrecht: Springer.

Hanson, F. A. (1993). *Testing testing: Social consequences of the examined life*. Los Angeles: University of California Press.

Harlen, W. (2006). The role of assessment in developing motivation for learning. In J. Gardner (Ed.), *Assessment and learning* (pp. 61–80). London: Sage.

Harlen, W. (2008). Trusting teachers' judgements. In S. Swaffield (Ed.), *Unlocking assessment: Understanding for reflection and application* (pp. 138–153). London: Routledge.

Hodgen, J., & Webb, M. (2008). Questioning and dialogue. In S. Swaffield (Ed.), *Unlocking assessment: Understanding for reflection and application* (pp. 73–89). London: Routledge.

Holloway, J. H. (2000). A value-added view of pupil performance. *Educational Leadership*, 57(5), 84–85.

Hull, G., & Schultz, K. (2002). *School's out! Bridging out-of-school literacies with classroom practice*. New York: Teachers College Press.

James, M. (2006). Assessment, teaching and theories of learning. In J. Gardner (Ed.), *Assessment and learning* (pp. 47–60). London: Sage.

James, M. (2008). Assessment and learning. In S. Swaffield (Ed.), *Unlocking assessment: Understanding for reflection and application* (pp. 20–35). London: Routledge.

Johnston, P. H., & Nicholls, J. G. (1995). Voices we want to hear and voices we don't. *Theory into Practice, 34*(2), 94–100.

Jones, A. (1991). *"At school I've got a chance". Culture/privilege: Pacific Islands and Pakeha girls at schools.* Palmerston North: Dunmore Press.

Kirkwood, M. (2007). The contribution of sustainable assessment to teachers' continuing professional development. In D. Boud & N. Falchikov (Eds.), *Rethinking assessment in higher education: Learning for the longer term* (pp. 167–180). London: Routledge.

Klenowski, V., Askew, S., & Carnell, E. (2006). Portfolios for learning, assessment and professional development. *Assessment in Higher Education, 31*(3), 267–286.

Kozulin, A., & Presseisen, B. Z. (1995). Mediated learning experience and psychological tools: Vygotsky's and Feuerstein's perspectives in a study of student learning. *Educational Psychologist, 30*(2), 67–75.

Kusnic, E., & Finley, M. L. (1993). Student self-evaluation: An introduction and rationale. *New Directions for Teaching and Learning, 56*(Winter), 5–13.

Kvale, S. (1996). *InterViews: An introduction to qualitative research interviewing.* Thousand Oaks, CA: Sage.

Kvale, S. (2007). Contradictions of assessment for learning in institutions of higher learning. In D. Boud & N. Falchikov (Eds.), *Rethinking assessment in higher education: Learning for the long term* (pp. 57–71). London: Routledge.

Lampert, M., Rittenhouse, P., & Crumbaugh, C. (1996). Agreeing to disagree: Developing sociable mathematical discourse. In D. R. Olson & N. Torrance (Eds.), *The handbook of education and human development* (pp. 731–764). Oxford: Blackwell.

Lave, J. (1988). *Cognition in practice. Mind, mathematics and culture in everyday life.* New York: Cambridge University Press.

Lave, J. (1996). Teaching, as learning, in practice. *Mind, Culture, and Activity: An International Journal, 3*(3), 149–164.

Lave, J., Murtaugh, M., & de la Rocha, O. (1984). The dialectic of arithmetic in grocery shopping. In B. Rogoff & J. Lave (Eds.), *Everyday cognition: Its development in social context* (pp. 67–94). Cambridge, MA: Harvard University Press.

Lave, J., & Wenger, E. (1991). *Situated learning: Legitimate peripheral participation.* Cambridge: Cambridge University Press.

Linn, R. L. (2003). Accountability: Responsibility and reasonable expectations. *Educational Researcher, 32*(7), 3–13.

Linn, R. L. (2004). Accountability models. In S. Fuhrman & R. Elmore (Eds.), *Redesigning accountability* (pp. 73–93). New York: Teachers College Press.

Locke, J. (1977). *An essay concerning human understanding. An abridgement.* London: J. M. Dent. (Original work published 1911.)

Loughran, J. (2002). Teacher as researcher: The PAVOT project. In J. Loughran, I. Mitchell, & J. Mitchell (Eds.), *Learning from teacher research* (pp. 3–18). Crows Nest, NSW: Allen & Unwin.

Loughran, J., & Northfield, J. (1996). *Opening the classroom door: Teacher, researcher, learner*. London: Falmer Press.

Martino, W., & Pallotta-Chiarolli, M. (2007). Schooling, normalisation, and gendered bodies: Adolescent boys' and girls' experiences of gender and schooling. In D. Thiessen & A. Cook-Sather (Eds.), *International handbook of student experience in elementary and secondary school* (pp. 346–374). Dordrecht: Springer.

Marton, F. (1981). Phenomenography: Describing conceptions of the world around us. *Instructional Science, 10*, 177–200.

Marton, F. (1986). Phenomenography: A research approach to investigating different understandings of reality. *Journal of Thought, 21*, 28–49.

Marton, F. (1988). Phenomenography: A research approach to investigating different understandings of reality. In R. R. Sherman & R. B. Webb (Eds.), *Qualitative research in education: Focus and methods* (pp. 141–161). London: Falmer Press.

Marton, F., & Booth, S. (1996). The learner's experience of learning. In D. R. Olson & N. Torrance (Eds.), *The handbook of education and human development* (pp. 534–564). Oxford: Blackwell.

Marton, F., & Booth, S. (1997). *Learning and awareness*. Mahwah, NJ: Lawrence Erlbaum.

Marton, F., Dall'Alba, G., & Beaty, E. (1993). Conceptions of learning. *International Journal of Educational Research, 19*(3), 277–300.

Marton, F., & Säljö, R. (1976). On qualitative differences in learning: I. Outcome and process. *British Journal of Educational Psychology, 46*, 4–11.

Marton, F., & Svensson, L. (1979). Conceptions of research in student learning. *Higher Education, 8*, 471–486.

Mattison, C. (1989). *Lizards of the world*. London: Blandford.

Matusov, E., Bell, N., & Rogoff, B. (2002). Schooling as cultural process: Working together and guidance by children from schools differing in collaborative practices. In R. V. Kail & H. W. Reese (Eds.), *Advances in child development and behavior* (Vol. 29, pp. 129–160). New York: Academic Press.

McCrudden, M. T., & Corkill, A. J. (2010). Verbal ability and the processing of scientific text with seductive detail sentences. *Reading Psychology, 31*(3), 282–300.

McNamee, G., & Sivright, S. (2002). Community supports for writing development among urban African American children. In G. Hull & K. Schultz (Eds.), *School's out! Bridging out-of-school literacies with classroom practice* (pp. 169–197). New York: Teachers College Press.

Méard, J., Bertone, S., & Flavier, E. (2008). How second-grade students internalize rules during teacher–student transactions: A case study. *British Journal of Educational Psychology, 78*, 395–410.

Metcalf, L. E., & Hunt, M. P. (1974). Relevance and the curriculum. In E. W. Eisner & E. Vallance (Eds.), *Conflicting conceptions of the curriculum* (pp. 136–146). Berkeley, CA: McCutchan.

Ministry of Education. (2007). *The New Zealand curriculum framework*. Wellington: Learning Media.

Ministry of Education. (2008). *Schools Plus discussion paper*. Wellington: Author.

Mitra, D. L. (2004). The significance of students: Can increasing student voice in schools lead to gains in youth development? *Teachers College Record, 4*, 651–688.

Moll, L. C., & Whitmore, K. F. (1993). Vygotsky in classroom practice: Moving from individual transmission to social transaction. In E. A. Forman, N. Minick, & C. A. Stone (Eds.), *Contexts for learning: Sociocultural dynamics in children's development* (pp. 19–42). New York: Oxford University Press.

Morss, J. R. (1996). *Growing critical: Alternatives to developmental psychology.* London: Routledge.

Nash, R. (1997). *Inequality/difference: A sociology of education.* Palmerston North: ERDC Press.

Neisser, U. (1982). Memory: What are the important questions? In U. Neisser (Ed.), *Memory observed: Remembering in natural contexts* (pp. 3–21). San Francisco: W. H. Freeman.

New Zealand Treasury. (2008, April). *Working smarter: Driving productivity growth through skills.* Retrieved from http://www.treasury.govt.nz/publications/research-policy/tprp/08-06/tprp08-06.pdf

Nichols, B. W., & Singer, K. P. (2000). Developing data mentors. *Educational Leadership, 57*(5), 34–37.

Nicholls, J., & Hazzard, S. (1993). *Education as adventure: Lessons from the second grade.* New York: Teachers College Press.

Nisbet, J. (1993). Introduction. In J. Nisbet (Ed.), *Curriculum reform: Assessment in question* (pp. 25–38). Paris: OECD.

Nisbet, J. (1994). Relating pupil assessment and evaluation to teaching and learning. In P. Highes (Ed.), *The curriculum redefined: Schooling for the 21st century* (pp. 165–169). Paris: OECD.

Noyce, P., Perda, D., & Traver, R. (2000). Creating data-driven schools. *Educational Leadership, 57*(5), 52–56.

Nuthall, G. (1999). The way students learn: Acquiring knowledge from an integrated science and social studies unit. *The Elementary School Journal, 99*(4), 303–342.

Nuthall, G. (2007). *The hidden lives of learners.* Wellington: NZCER Press.

O'Neill, O. (2002). *A question of trust.* Cambridge: Cambridge University Press.

Organisation for Economic Co-operation and Development. (2006). *Education at a glance: OECD indicators (2006).* Centre for Educational Research and Innovation. Paris: OECD. [Press release 12.09.06] Retrieved from http://www.oecd.org/document/4/0.3343.en 2649 34487 37387877 1 1 1 1 .00.html

Packer, M. J., & Goicoechea, J. (2000). Sociocultural and constructivist theories of learning: Ontology, not just epistemology. *Educational Psychologist, 35*(4), 227–241

Paley, V. G. (1979). *White teacher.* Cambridge, MA: Harvard University Press.

Paley, V. G. (1999). *The kindness of children.* Cambridge, MA: Harvard University Press.

Perkins, D. (1995). *Outsmarting IQ: The emerging science of learnable intelligence.* New York: The Free Press.

Petrone, R. (2010). "You have to get hit a couple of times": The role of conflict in learning how to "be" a skateboarder. *Teaching and Teacher Education, 26,* 119–127.

Piaget, J. (1929). *The child's conception of the world.* New York: Harcourt, Brace & World.

Piaget, J. (1979). *Science of education and the psychology of the child.* New York: Penguin. (Originally published 1969.)

Pollard, A. (1997). *Reflective teaching in the primary school: A handbook for the classroom* (3rd ed.). London: Cassell.

Pollard, A., Broadfoot, P., Croll, P., Osborn, M., & Abbott, D. (1994). *Changing English primary schools? The impact of the Education Reform Act at Key Stage One.* London: Cassell.
Pramling, I. (1983). *The child's conceptions of learning.* Göteborg: University of Göteborg.
Pramling, I. (1988). Developing children's thinking about their own learning. *British Journal of Educational Psychology, 58,* 266–278.
Pramling, I. (1990). *Learning to learn: A study of Swedish preschool children.* New York: Springer-Verlag.
Pramling, I. (1996). Understanding and empowering the child as learner. In D. R. Olson & N. Torrance (Eds.), *The handbook of education and human development* (pp. 565–592). Oxford: Blackwell.
Pramling, I., Asplund Carlsson, M., & Klerfelt, A. (1993, September). *Children's understanding of a tale.* Paper presented at the Conference on Issues in Australian Childhood, Brisbane.
Raider-Roth, M. B. (2005). *Trusting what you know: The high stakes of classroom relationships.* San Francisco: Jossey-Bass.
Ramsden, P. (Ed.). (1988). *Improving learning: New perspectives.* London: Kogan Page.
Resnick, L. B. (1987). *Education and learning to think.* Washington, DC: National Academy Press.
Rogoff, B. (1990). *Apprenticeship in thinking: Cognitive development in social context.* Oxford: Oxford University Press.
Rogoff, B. (1997). Evaluating development in the process of participation: Theory, methods, and practice building on each other. In E. Amsel & A. Renninger (Eds.), *Change and development* (pp. 265–285). Hillsdale, NJ: Erlbaum.
Rogoff, B. (1998). Cognition as a collaborative process. In W. Damon (Series Ed.) & D. Kuhn & R. S. Siegler (Vol. Eds.), *Handbook of child psychology: Vol 2. Cognition, perception, and language* (pp. 679–744). New York: Wiley.
Rogoff, B. (2003). *The cultural nature of human development.* New York: Oxford University Press.
Rogoff, B., & Lave, J. (1984). *Everyday cognition: Its development in social context.* Cambridge, MA: Harvard University Press.
Rogoff, B., Matusov, M., & White, C. (1996). Models of teaching and learning: Participation in a community of learners. In D. R. Olson & N. Torrance (Eds.), *The handbook of education and human development* (pp. 388–414). Oxford: Blackwell.
Rogoff, B., & Mistry, J. (1990). The social and functional context of children's remembering. In R. Fivush & J. A. Hudson (Eds.), *Knowing and remembering in young children* (pp. 197–222). Cambridge: Cambridge University Press.
Rogoff, B., Mistry, J., Göncü, A., & Mosier, C. (1993). Guided participation in cultural activity by toddlers and caregivers. *Monographs of the Society for Research in Child Development, 58*(7, Serial No. 236).
Rogoff, B. Moore, L., Najafi, B., Dexter, A., Correa-Chavez, M., & Solis, J. (2007). Children's development of cultural repertoires through participation in everyday routines and practices. In J. E. Grusec & P. D. Hastings (Eds.), *Handbook of socialization* (pp. 490–515). New York: Guildford.
Rogoff, B., Paradise, R., Mejía Arauz, R., Correa-Chávez, M., & Angelillo, C. (2003). Firsthand learning through intent participation. *Annual Review of Psychology, 54,* 175–203.

Rogoff, B., & Toma, C. (1997). Shared thinking: Community and institutional variations. *Discourse Processes, 23,* 471–497.

Rosner, J. (2003). On white preferences. *The Nation, 276*(14), 24.

Ross, J. A., & Starling, M. (2008). Self-assessment in a technology-supported environment: The case of grade 9 geography. *Assessment in Education: Principles, Policy & Practice, 15*(2), 183–199.

Rudduck, J. (2007). Student voice, student engagement, and school reform. In D. Thiessen & A. Cook-Sather (Eds.), *International handbook of student experience in elementary and secondary school* (pp. 589–610). Dordrecht: Springer.

Rudduck, J., & McIntyre, D. (2007). *Improving learning through consulting pupils.* London: Routledge.

Sadler, P. M., & Good, E. (2006). The impact of self- and peer-grading on student learning. *Educational Assessment, 11*(1), 1–31.

Säljö, R. (1979). *Learning in the learner's perspective. I. Some common-sense conceptions.* Göteborg: Göteborg University.

Säljö, R. (1996). Minding action: Conceiving of the world versus participating in cultural practices. In G. Dall'Alba & B. Hasselgren (Eds.), *Reflections on phenomenography: Towards a methodology?* (pp. 19–34). Göteborg: Acta Universitatis Gothoburgensis.

Säljö, R., & Wyndhamn, J. (1993). Solving everyday problems in the formal setting: An empirical study of the school as context for thought. In S. Chaiklin & J. Lave (Eds.), *Understanding practice: Perspectives on activity and context* (pp. 327–342). Cambridge: Cambridge University Press.

Shor, I. (1992). *Empowering education: Critical teaching for social change.* Chicago: University of Chicago Press.

Skilton-Sylvester, E. (2002). Literate at home but not at school. In G. Hull & K. Schultz (Eds.), *School's out! Bridging out-of-school illiteracies with classroom practice* (pp. 61–90). New York: Teachers College Press.

Skinner, B. F. (1972). *Beyond freedom and dignity.* London: Jonathan Cape.

Smyth, J. (2007). Toward the pedagogically engaged school: Listening to student voice as a positive response to disengagement and 'dropping out'? In D. Thiessen & A. Cook-Sather (Eds.), *International handbook of student experience in elementary and secondary school* (pp. 635–658). Dordrecht: Springer.

Solomon, J. (1994). Towards a notion of home culture: Science education in the home. *British Educational Research Journal, 20*(5), 565–577.

Sperling, D. (1993). What's worth an 'A'? Setting standards together. *Educational Leadership, 50*(5), 73–75.

Stenhouse, L. (1981). What counts as research? *British Journal of Education Studies, 29*(2), 103–114.

Stevenson, L. (2008). *Personalised learning in a Web 2.0 environment.* Unpublished Master's thesis, University of Waikato, Hamilton. Available online at http://hdl.handle.net/10289/2377

Stipek, D., Recchia, S., & McClintic, S. (1992). Self evaluation in young children. *Monographs of the Society for Research in Child Development, 57*(1, Serial No. 226).

Svensson, L. (1994, November). Theoretical foundations of phenomenography. In *Phenomenography: Philosophy and practice* (pp. 9–20). Brisbane: Queensland University of Technology.

Tan, K. (2007). Conceptions of self-assessment: What is needed for long-term learning? In D. Boud & N. Falchikov (Eds.), *Rethinking assessment in higher education: Learning for the long term* (pp. 114–127). London: Routledge.

Thiessen, D., & Cook-Sather, A. (Eds.). (2007). *International handbook of student experience in elementary and secondary school*. Dordrecht: Springer.

Thrupp, M., & Smith, R. (1999). A decade of ERO. *New Zealand Journal of Educational Studies, 34*(1), 186–198.

van Kraayenoord, C. E., & Paris, S. G. (1997). Australian students' self-appraisal of their work samples and academic progress. *Elementary School Journal, 97*(5), 523–537.

Vygotsky, L. S. (1978). *Mind in society*. Cambridge, MA: Harvard University Press.

Vygotsky, L. S. (1981). The genesis of higher mental functions. In J. V. Wertsch (Ed.), *The concept of activity in Soviet psychology* (pp. 144–188). New York: M. E. Sharpe.

Vygotsky, L. S. (1988). The genesis of higher mental functions. In K. Richardson & S. Sheldon (Eds.), *Cognitive development to adolescence* (pp. 61–80). London: Lawrence Erlbaum.

Wiliam, D. (2006). Formative assessment: Getting the focus right. *Educational Assessment, 11*(3 & 4), 283–289.

Wiliam, D. (2010). Standardized testing and school accountability. *Educational Psychologist, 45*(2), 107–122.

Wood, D. J., Bruner, J. S., & Ross, G. (1976). The role of tutoring in problem solving. *Journal of Child Psychology and Psychiatry, 17*, 89–100.

Woods, P. (1990). *The happiest days? How pupils cope with school*. London: Falmer Press.

Wortham, S. E. F. (2006). *Learning identity: The joint emergence of social identification and academic learning*. New York: Cambridge University Press.

Zajac, R. J., & Hartup, W. N. (1997). Friends as coworkers: Research review and classroom implications. *Elementary School Journal, 98*(1), 3–13.

www.ingramcontent.com/pod-product-compliance
Lightning Source LLC
Chambersburg PA
CBHW081331230426
43667CB00018B/2897